Factory Farming

Other Books in the Current Controversies Series

Factory Farming

Debra A. Miller, Book Editor

GREENHAVEN PRESS
A part of Gale, Cengage Learning

Detroit • New York • San Francisco • New Haven, Conn • Waterville, Maine • London

GALE
CENGAGE Learning·

Elizabeth Des Chenes, *Director, Publishing Solutions*

© 2013 Greenhaven Press, a part of Gale, Cengage Learning

Gale and Greenhaven Press are registered trademarks used herein under license.

For more information, contact:
Greenhaven Press
27500 Drake Rd.
Farmington Hills, MI 48331-3535
Or you can visit our Internet site at gale.cengage.com

For product information and technology assistance, contact us at

Gale Customer Support, 1-800-877-4253
For permission to use material from this text or product, submit all requests online at
www.cengage.com/permissions

Further permissions questions can be emailed to permissionrequest@cengage.com

Articles in Greenhaven Press anthologies are often edited for length to meet page require-ments. In addition, original titles of these works are changed to clearly present the main thesis and to explicitly indicate the author's opinion. Every effort is made to ensure that Greenhaven Press accurately reflects the original intent of the authors. Every effort has been made to trace the owners of copyrighted material.

Cover image copyright © branislapudar/ShutterStock.com.

LIBRARY OF CONGRESS CATALOGING-IN-PUBLICATION DATA

Factory farming / Debra A. Miller, book editor.
   p. cm. -- (Current controversies)
   Includes bibliographical references and index.
   ISBN 978-0-7377-6872-5 (hardcover) -- ISBN 978-0-7377-6873-2 (paperback)
   1. Factory farms. 2. Factory farms--Social aspects. 3. Factory farms--Moral and ethical aspects. 4. Factory farms--Environmental aspects. I. Miller, Debra A.
   SF140.L58F332 2013
   636'.01--dc23
                                                                        2013003129

Printed in the United States of America
   1 2 3 4 5   17 16 15 14 13

Contents

Chapter 1: Is Factory Farming Needed to Feed the World?

Yes: Factory Farming Is Needed to Feed the World

No: Factory Farming Is Not Needed to Feed the World

By eliminating many of the factory farming methods that are destroying the environment and human health and allowing animals to feed on grasses instead of grains, organic farming can produce enough food to feed the world. Sustainable farming practices can also help reduce world poverty.

Chapter 2: Is Factory Farming an Ethical Way to Treat Animals?

The truth underlying factory farming is that, as a business, it maximizes profits by treating animals as commodities rather than as sentient beings that experience pain and sadness. The methods used to raise and slaughter chickens, pigs, and beef and dairy cattle, and to produce milk and eggs are cruel, unhealthy, and inhumane.

One idea for improving factory farms is to remove the cerebral cortex of chickens in order to remove the animals' sense perceptions, so that they can be kept alive and grown in denser conditions without feeling pain or stress. The demand for meat is increasing rapidly; this could resolve some of the ethical problems associated with factory farming of meat while creating others.

Foreword

By definition, controversies are "discussions of questions in which opposing opinions clash" (*Webster's Twentieth Century Dictionary Unabridged*). Few would deny that controversies are a pervasive part of the human condition and exist on virtually every level of human enterprise. Controversies transpire between individuals and among groups, within nations and between nations. Controversies supply the grist necessary for progress by providing challenges and challengers to the status quo. They also create atmospheres where strife and warfare can flourish. A world without controversies would be a peaceful world; but it also would be, by and large, static and prosaic.

The Series' Purpose

The purpose of the Current Controversies series is to explore many of the social, political, and economic controversies dominating the national and international scenes today. Titles selected for inclusion in the series are highly focused and specific. For example, from the larger category of criminal justice, Current Controversies deals with specific topics such as police brutality, gun control, white collar crime, and others. The debates in Current Controversies also are presented in a useful, timeless fashion. Articles and book excerpts included in each title are selected if they contribute valuable, long-range ideas to the overall debate. And wherever possible, current information is enhanced with historical documents and other relevant materials. Thus, while individual titles are current in focus, every effort is made to ensure that they will not become quickly outdated. Books in the Current Controversies series will remain important resources for librarians, teachers, and students for many years.

In addition to keeping the titles focused and specific, great care is taken in the editorial format of each book in the series. Book introductions and chapter prefaces are offered to provide background material for readers. Chapters are organized around several key questions that are answered with diverse opinions representing all points on the political spectrum. Materials in each chapter include opinions in which authors clearly disagree as well as alternative opinions in which authors may agree on a broader issue but disagree on the possible solutions. In this way, the content of each volume in Current Controversies mirrors the mosaic of opinions encountered in society. Readers will quickly realize that there are many viable answers to these complex issues. By questioning each author's conclusions, students and casual readers can begin to develop the critical thinking skills so important to evaluating opinionated material.

Current Controversies is also ideal for controlled research. Each anthology in the series is composed of primary sources taken from a wide gamut of informational categories including periodicals, newspapers, books, US and foreign government documents, and the publications of private and public organizations. Readers will find factual support for reports, debates, and research papers covering all areas of important issues. In addition, an annotated table of contents, an index, a book and periodical bibliography, and a list of organizations to contact are included in each book to expedite further research.

Perhaps more than ever before in history, people are confronted with diverse and contradictory information. During the Persian Gulf War, for example, the public was not only treated to minute-to-minute coverage of the war, it was also inundated with critiques of the coverage and countless analyses of the factors motivating US involvement. Being able to sort through the plethora of opinions accompanying today's major issues, and to draw one's own conclusions, can be a complicated and frustrating struggle. It is the editors' hope that Current Controversies will help readers with this struggle.

Introduction

> *"Today, most meats and other foods sold in the United States and abroad are produced by large corporations using mass production techniques designed to maximize profits and keep consumer costs low."*

For centuries, farms around the world were mostly small operations, which were owned and run by rural families and produced various plant and animal food products for local markets. On these small farms, fields were planted with different vegetable, fruit, and grain crops. A variety of animals were commonly raised on these farms as well: cows in open pastures, pigs in muddy pens, and free-roaming chickens in yards. Modern farming practices, however, are very different from this farm past.

Today, most meats and other foods sold in the United States and abroad are produced by large corporations using mass production techniques designed to maximize profits and keep consumer costs low. Most large crop farms owned by agribusiness corporations spread over thousands of acres, produce just a few commodity crops (such as corn, soybeans, and wheat), and use industrial practices such as large machines and chemical fertilizers and pesticides. Similarly, modern corporate-owned livestock, dairy, and chicken/egg producers raise thousands of farm animals inside huge buildings, injecting them with antibiotics to prevent disease and feeding them vitamin-rich foods and supplements to make them grow or produce quickly. These modern industrial farms are generally referred to as factory farms, but the term *factory farm* is often used as a negative label to refer exclusively to big farm animal operations, sites that are also called concentrated animal feeding operations (CAFOs). For good or bad, by the early 2000s large factory farms had largely replaced smaller family farms. According to Worldwatch Institute, factory farms are the source of 74 percent of the world's poultry, 68 percent of eggs, 50 percent of pork, and 43 percent of beef.

Although widespread, factory farming is a recent phenomenon. Industrial farming of crops, for example, was made possible only as a result of intensive farming methods and other discoveries made during and after the Industrial Revolution, a period from 1750 to 1850 when many western countries shifted from human and animal labor to machines and mass production. In the 1800s, for example, a number of farm machines were invented to help farmers plant, harvest, and process crops. Later, improvements in shipping such as refrigerated railroad cars enabled farmers to ship their meat products to remote markets. Another innovation in the nineteenth century was the discovery of the role of nitrogen and phosphorus in stimulating plant growth. In the twentieth century, crop farming benefited dramatically when petroleum-based chemicals, developed for use in World War II (1939–1945), were used to produce pesticides, herbicides, and synthetic fertilizers for American farmers. These petrochemical products, together with advances in genetics and irrigation, helped launch the green revolution, a transformation in agriculture characterized by larger US farms and dramatic increases in agricultural productivity that helped to feed a growing world population.

The green revolution's production of cheap grains, in turn, led to larger animal agriculture farms and allowed more people to eat meat and meat products than ever before. Chickens were the first farm animal to be factory farmed, partly due to the discovery of the role of vitamins in animal nutrition in the 1920s. When vitamins A and D are added to feed, animals do not require sunlight, and they can be housed indoors. By the 1970s, giant egg production companies became the norm. Next, the development of antibiotics and vaccines caused animals to grow faster and helped meat producers better control diseases that spread among animals raised in dense conditions. These innovations led to the growth of massive pig farms in southern states such as North Carolina during the 1960s. This trend continued through the decades with the rise of large dairy, turkey, and cattle operations. In recent years, animal genetic research, selective breeding, and growth hormones have added to the output of factory farms, for example, by producing cows that produce more milk and faster growing, meatier chickens, turkeys, and pigs. In each area of animal production, these factory farms squeezed out smaller farms and led to consolidation of companies so that by the early 2000s only a few mega-corporations controlled almost all of the market.

Consumers appreciate the cheap prices made possible by factory farms, but these operations face growing criticism from environmentalists, safe food proponents, and animal rights activists. Critics charge that this industrial system, especially animal production, is environmentally unsustainable because it produces unchecked air and water pollution due to the overuse of chemicals and the release of huge amounts of concentrated animal waste. Health advocates complain about antibiotics used in animal production, arguing that these drugs are now so widespread in the environment that they are becoming ineffective as medicine. Food advocates claim that pesticides in factory farmed fruits and vegetables and hormones in meat are not safe for human consumption. In addition, animal rights supporters have increasingly challenged the ways that factory farms house and slaughter farm animals, charging that they are inhumane and subject sentient animals to constant suffering.

Supporters of modern farming methods believe that industrial techniques are the only way to produce enough food to feed the global population. They cite improvements that they are making in areas such as animal welfare and the environment and argue that critics simply do not understand farming or the competitive pressures facing modern farms. A growing number of agriculture researchers, however, conclude that agriculture must move toward a smaller, more sustainable model of farming in coming decades. These experts assert that by employing advanced organic and sustainable agricultural techniques at a local level, small farms could be fully capable of producing the quantities of food needed for the world's growing population without destroying the environment or mistreating animals. The authors of the viewpoints included in *Current Controversies: Factory Farming* address some of the issues surrounding the debate about factory farms, including whether factory farming truly is needed to feed the world's population and whether it is an ethical way to treat animals. The viewpoints also discuss how much factory farming harms the environment and human health and what role it will play in the future of food production.

CHAPTER 1

Is Factory Farming Needed to Feed the World?

Chapter Preface

One of the central questions in agriculture in the early 2000s is whether food producers will be able to feed the world's growing population over the next fifty years. The global population as of mid-2011 was just over seven billion, and that number was expected to grow to about 9.2 billion by 2050. Some estimates suggest that population growth may decline thereafter due to increased living standards and accompanying lower birth rates, but typically higher standards of living mean higher consumption of meat, which in turn requires more grain production. In fact, according to the United Nations (UN) Food and Agricultural Organization (FAO), population growth combined with higher living standards was anticipated to require global food production to increase by 70 percent to meet the projected demand for food as of 2050. Whether and how this demand can be met is a subject of serious debate.

The world actually has faced this dilemma before. As early as 1798, British political economist Thomas R. Malthus (1766–1834) saw a link between population growth and famine and predicted that a growing human population could exceed the food supply. Similar concerns were expressed in the early 1900s when world population began spiking, but instead of a dwindling supply, a so-called green revolution, fueled by chemical pesticides and herbicides developed during World War II (1939–1945) along with other agricultural advances, produced remarkable increases in world crop production. Grain output, in particular, rose dramatically, especially in Asia where rice is a staple food item. High-yielding varieties of other grains also were developed, including corn, wheat, and soybeans. The result was that more than enough food was produced to feed the world; the per person production of food actually increased despite the huge population increase.

The green revolution may have been a huge success in terms of food production, but it came with certain serious drawbacks. The main negative was that it required industrial production techniques such as massive applications of chemical fertilizers, pesticides, and herbicides; heavy use of fresh water; a focus on a small number of high-yield crop and animal species; and abusive conditions for farm animals. Further, this method of farming, many experts say, is not sustainable over the long run because it depletes the soils, requires increasing amounts of chemical inputs, causes environmental contamination, and is destructive of biodiversity and habitat for other plants and animals.

Despite these environmental and other concerns, many agriculture researchers are calling for a second green revolution to meet expected food demand as the world population grows by more than two billion people in coming decades. A second green revolution will be more difficult, however, because it would face constraints not present in the 1950s and 1960s. For example, most of the world's productive, arable land in the early 2000s had already been exploited for agriculture. Arable land accounts for only about 10 percent of the global land area, and the rest composed of forests (including tropical rainforests), deserts, urban areas, or land that is not suitable for agriculture for various other reasons. In addition, the supplies of fresh water needed for agriculture are diminishing because they are increasingly used for urban areas, redirected to industry, or polluted by environmentally hazardous activities. These difficulties are compounded by the potential effects of climate change, which are expected to cause prolonged droughts, torrential rains, and a myriad of other weather changes that will likely present huge challenges for agriculture in the future. Already, in the summer of 2012, US farmers faced record droughts that were expected to reduce US corn production by 17 percent, an event that many experts see as a harbinger of things to come for farmers.

Thus, it is anticipated that farmers in the future will not be able to increase productivity through land expansion or better irrigation; they will be limited to increasing yields in other ways while facing many more challenges. Optimists suggest that crop yields can be achieved through technological advances such as genetic engineering and faster breeding, which will develop varieties of plants—possibly even perennial grains—that will be able to grow with less water and in poor soil conditions and that will make better use of artificial or natural fertilizers. Other agriculture improvements such as better pest management, water-conserving irrigation, and conservation tillage could also play important roles.

Another question is whether the need for food will make the factory farm model of industrial food production a necessity or whether the increases in production can be accomplished in a more environmentally sustainable and animal-friendly method, through the use of organic or small farm agriculture methods. The authors of the viewpoints in this chapter state their views on whether factory farming is needed to feed the world.

Factory Farming Is Essential to Feed the World

David Leyonhjelm

David Leyonhjelm is registered officer of the Liberal Democratic Party in Australia. He also works in the agribusiness and veterinary markets there.

A report issued last month [December 2011] by the UN [United Nations] Food and Agriculture Organisation says intensive livestock production will be essential to meet increased demand for animal protein over the next four decades.

More Meat Needed in the Future

Projections for population growth and a rise in per capita consumption of animal protein in developing countries mean that the world will be consuming two-thirds more animal protein in 2050 than it does today. The report estimates meat consumption will rise by 73% and dairy consumption by 58% over current levels.

The last forty-five years has seen a significant increase in world animal protein production. Since 1967 global production of poultry meat has increased by around 700%, eggs by 350%, pig meat by 290%, sheep and goat meat by 200%, beef and buffalo meat by 180% and milk by 180%. Livestock are increasingly important to the food security of millions of people.

To maintain these rates of growth for another four decades would require a further doubling of poultry numbers, 80% more sheep and goats, 50% more cattle and 40% more pigs.

The report points out that there are no technically or economically viable alternatives to large scale, intensive production for the bulk of the livestock-derived food required in the cities, where virtually all the population growth will occur.

Given limits on the availability of land, water, waste disposal and other resources, significant increases in productivity will be needed, requiring significant capital investment plus encouragement from policymakers and regulators.

The term factory farming is accurate. If a factory means efficient, large scale production, then that is what it is.

The definition of increased productivity is a higher ratio of outputs to inputs. In other words, more milk, meat and eggs must be produced using less than a corresponding increase in feed, labour and other components of production.

In practical terms that means larger numbers of animals managed by fewer people, using genetically superior livestock and modern technology to keep the animals healthy and productive. It is the exact opposite of the low-tech, small holdings that typified the last century, still prevalent in developing countries but increasingly restricted to hobby farms and luxury niche producers in Australia and other developed countries.

It is also the exact opposite of what those who use the term factory farming to describe modern livestock production would like to see.

Factory Farms Are Necessary and Humane

By some measures the term factory farming is accurate. If a factory means efficient, large scale production, then that is what it is. The largest farms house millions of chickens or hundreds of thousands of pigs or cattle. The capital value of the livestock and facilities is counted in tens of millions of dollars.

Obviously there is no place for naming each animal or treating them as pets. Trucks deliver tonnes of feed on a daily basis, which is served up to the animals by conveyor. Animals are mass vaccinated and medicated using multi injectors, water medication, aerosols or in-feed treatments.

But those who use the term intend it to be derogatory. They either believe that intensive, large-scale production is inherently cruel or that eating animals is fundamentally wrong. Either way, they advocate a return to the small-scale farming of half a century ago.

They claim chickens are unbearably crammed together in a soup of ammonia and faeces, unable to engage in natural behaviours, forced to grow at unnatural rates, crammed with antibiotics and slaughtered under inhumane conditions. Turkeys are said to endure painful beak trimming, overcrowding and the effects of excessive growth rates. Egg laying chickens are said to suffer unspeakably in cages.

On pig production they claim sows reproduce in inhumane conditions and, along with their piglets, are forced to live on concrete and suffer painful procedures.

If the animals were suffering from the unspeakable cruelties so often attributed to factory farming, they would be dying like flies.

By implication it is assumed that chickens, turkeys and pigs feel the same about these things as if they were humans.

Like all effective propaganda, such criticisms of factory farming are close enough to the truth to appear believable. By using selective examples and representing exceptions as representative, with frequent and eloquent repetition, they are regularly accepted as facts. Politicians and policy makers, often with no better information of their own, are tempted to regulate in the belief that there is a problem requiring a solution. Such "solutions" have the potential to deny food security to millions of people.

There Is No Problem

In fact there is no problem. Livestock farmers do not make money unless they take proper care of their animals. In many ways factory farming is more humane than the small scale farming of old.

Chickens receive a perfectly balanced diet to which they have constant access. They also have plentiful water, are protected from wind, rain, heat and cold, and are safe from foxes, snakes and insects. To the extent that technology allows, everything is done to ensure they lead a stress and disease-free life. Indeed, the avoidance of stress and disease is the top priority.

The ammonia emitted by chicken faeces is no problem unless the chickens are sick, which is rarely the case. Antibiotics are expensive and thus used sparingly. Growth defects only occur if the diet is unbalanced. Beaks may be trimmed to prevent pecking of other birds but does not inhibit eating or growth. Stocking densities cannot be too high or they would inhibit growth rates and cause other problems.

Fairly obviously, if the animals were suffering from the unspeakable cruelties so often attributed to factory farming, they would be dying like flies rather than contentedly eating and growing or producing eggs.

As for pigs, reproductive efficiency and growth rates have soared in recent decades, obvious evidence that their housing and management are of more concern to the critics than the pigs. An important contributor has been housing that prevents the sows from crushing tiny piglets.

Indeed, reproduction is one of the first things to decline when animals are suffering. The fact that pigs reproduce so prolifically and chickens lay eggs so plentifully gives the lie to the claims of the factory farming critics.

However romantic it may appear to middle class urban consumers in developed countries for chickens to be scratching around in the dust or pigs to be wallowing in the mud, this is not conducive to efficient production. Some will be willing to pay for the privilege of having their meat or eggs produced under such conditions, and no doubt some farmers will be happy to supply them.

But this is not an option for most of the world, and neither should it be imposed. Millions of people want to enjoy more meat, eggs and dairy products in their diet, including many now emerging from poverty. Whether they are permitted to enjoy them may depend on how much the policy makers and politicians are influenced by those who regard factory farming as a problem.

The Efficiencies of Factory Farming Are Necessary to Keep Prices Low and Prevent Starvation

Dan Murphy

Dan Murphy is a veteran food-industry journalist and commentator.

I encountered a typical complaint the other day, one that over the years I've heard more variations on than a chess master has openings.

"I don't really like to eat meat, because those animals are just so abused."

The speaker was an otherwise intelligent, well-educated young woman with enough smarts and savvy to have risen to the managerial ranks in her company at an age my biggest accomplishment was blowing my measly paycheck—and my weekend—on the futile pursuit of whatever girl du jour I had no chance of landing.

This particular young woman was a sucker for the "pumped full of antibiotics and hormones" rhetoric that anti-industry activists are so adept at disseminating. Even though she admits to being underweight and anemic, she vowed to gain her way back to a normal BMI [body mass index, relative percentages of fat and muscle mass] by increasing her consumption of—wait for it—peanut butter.

I'll grant you, George Washington Carver was a genius who created some 300 uses for the peanut, but none of his patents involved the reversal of anemia. Although highly nutritious, a jar of Skippy isn't going to take anyone to a place, nutritionally speaking, that lean meat can't go more efficiently and, truth be told, contributing far fewer calories and fat to one's diet (a single cup of peanut butter delivers more than 1,500 calories, two-thirds of them from fat).

It's just easier for the groups invested in promoting vegetarianism to attack producers on the confinement issue.

That's the predictable part of the discussion I had with this young woman. The interesting part, however, was that her objections to eating meat centered not on how animals are killed, but on how they lived. It's not about humane slaughter, it's about humane lifestyle, if that term can be properly applied to farm animals.

Interesting, because her objections echo the more recent positioning of the activist community. Ten years ago, there were high-profile campaigns against inhumane slaughter, and lots of accusations about animals being skinned alive and chickens getting manhandled at the plant, and pigs jammed into overheated trailers on their way to slaughter.

Those issues, however, have largely subsided, and for the past five years or so, the thrust of both the activist community's propaganda and its campaign funding has been focused squarely on living conditions, not slaughter. Thus, the referenda launched against gestation stalls and battery cages and veal crates, and the concurrent marketing of the benefits of free-range production, open housing systems and the outdoor access that many alternative agriculture participants preach to their customers.

Pushing Back on the Issues

In some ways, it's just easier for the groups invested in promoting vegetarianism to attack producers on the confinement issue. Most people still harbor romantic notions of a now non-existent farmstead with chickens running loose, a couple pigs covered in mud and a docile cow in the barn munching on hay as their conceptual framework for food production.

It's also a far better source of the angst activists prey on to drive their fund-raising, and focusing on living conditions allows those holier-then-thou groups to hide behind a reform banner, rather than admitting their ultimate goal is a meat-free society.

So how does the industry push back? On two fronts.

First, by pushing forward in the evolution of production systems that incorporate the key concerns consumers have about food animals: open, or group housing systems and access to the outdoors. In the end there is no inherent conflict, no technical barriers to adding those elements to production that cannot be overcome. Just the necessary determination and the appropriate investment.

Second, the looming specter of a world population plagued by food shortages—even in our own lifetime—represents a real awakening for the very people, like the young woman I spoke with, who are intelligent enough about the larger issues of resource limitations and climate change to appreciate the urgency of maintaining, if not increasing, global farm productivity.

There is fertile ground, I believe, to discuss the merits of so-called industrial agriculture. Without the efficiencies inherent in modern food production, there would be starvation in many places around the world. Although we like to believe that could never happen here, the specter of soaring food prices does hit home, and it's there that traction can be gained for establishing not just the justification for, but the necessity of factory farming.

I know activists love that phrase, but I think it's time for producers and farmers to demystify it and drain it of its pejorative context. Nobody objects to the *concept* of a factory, if—and that's a big if—the working conditions are satisfactory.

And few people complain about the concept of mechanized farming when it applies to commodities such as corn, wheat and soybeans. Heck, there wouldn't be a veggie activist alive today to protest production agriculture without the availability and affordability of soy protein in its many culinary incarnations.

It's only animals that are seen as victims in the farming and food production systems that have evolved so dramatically over the past 50 years.

And as long as industry maintains the efficiencies, and mitigates the deficiencies, there is no reason that even the more critical consumers can't be eventually persuaded to skip the Skippy and return to meat-eating.

Factory Farmed Fish Can Help to Feed an Expanding World Population

Worldwatch Institute

Worldwatch Institute is an independent research organization that advocates for a transition to a sustainable world that meets human needs.

Nearly half of the seafood we eat today is farmed. And while aquaculture is often equated with pollution, habitat degradation, and health risks, this explosive growth in fish farming may in fact be the most hopeful trend in the world's increasingly troubled food system, according to a new report by WorldWatch Institute [an environmental group].

In "Farming Fish for the Future," Senior Researcher Brian Halweil illustrates how, if properly guided, fish farming can not only help feed an expanding global population, but also play a role in healing marine ecosystems battered by overfishing.

"In a world where fresh water and grain supplies are increasingly scarce, raising seafood like oysters, clams, catfish, and tilapia is many times more efficient than factory-farmed chicken or beef," says Halweil. "Farmed fish can be a critical way to add to the global diet to hedge against potential crop losses or shortages in the supply of meat."

"But not all fish farming is created equal," Halweil notes. Carnivorous species like salmon and shrimp, while increasingly popular, consume several times their weight in fish feed—derived from other, typically smaller, fish—as they provide in edible seafood. "It generally requires 20 kilograms of feed to produce just 1 kilogram of tuna," Halweil says. "So even as we depend more on farmed fish, a growing scarcity of fish feed may jeopardize future expansion of the industry."

On average, each person on the planet is eating four times as much seafood as was consumed in 1950.

The Need for More Sustainable Fish Farms

Poorly run fish farms can generate coastal pollution in the form of excess feed and manure, and escaped fish and disease originating on farms can devastate wild fisheries. For example, a fish farm with 200,000 salmon releases nutrients and fecal matter roughly equivalent to the raw sewage generated by 20,000 to 60,000 people. Scotland's salmon aquaculture industry is estimated to produce the same amount of nitrogen waste as the untreated sewage of 3.2 million people—just over half the country's population.

Cramped facilities can also create ill health for fish, costing producers millions of dollars in disease prevention and foregone revenues. In recent years, shrimp farmers in China have lost $120 million to bacterial fish diseases and $420 million to shrimp diseases.

Fish farming has expanded to meet the soaring global demand for seafood. On average, each person on the planet is eating four times as much seafood as was consumed in 1950. The average per-capita consumption of farmed seafood has increased nearly 1,000 percent since 1970, in contrast to per-capita meat consumption, which grew just 60 percent.

In 2006, fish farmers raised nearly 70 million tons of seafood worth more than $80 billion—nearly double the volume of a decade earlier. Experts predict that farmed seafood will grow an additional 70 percent by 2030.

How can fish farming be made more sustainable? Innovative industry practices are key, but a shift toward sustainable fish farming will also require a fundamental change in public attitudes. This includes a willingness to prioritize fish that are lower on the food chain, such as shellfish and tilapia. But can consumers today be mobilized to shift the aquaculture industry in the same way they pressured tuna fleets to adopt more dolphin-friendly practices in the 1980s?

The need for more sustainable fish farming is critical, according to the report. Farmed seafood provides 42 percent of the world's seafood supply, and is on target to exceed half in the next decade, yet there are no widely accepted standards for what constitutes "good" fish farming. By comparison, the organic food industry has strong international and national standards, even though it constitutes just 3 to 5 percent of the world's food supply.

This points to a greater role for aquaculture certification and standards in the coming years, Halweil says. Efforts currently under way seek to model the effective labeling systems that exist in other areas of agriculture, such as for wild-caught fish, heritage breeds of livestock, and organic and local foods.

"The last wild ingredient in our diet is no longer completely wild," says Halweil. "This doesn't have to be a permanent situation, since wild fish stocks can recover. But as more coastal ecosystems are transformed into sites for fish pens, cages, and cultured seaweeds, fish farmers and the food industry will need to make ecological restoration as much a goal as meeting the growing demand for seafood."

The shellfish filter excess waste from the fish cages, while the seaweed thrives on dissolved nutrients in the water.

Innovations for Sustainability

Fortunately, not all fish farming is created equal. Rather than contributing to environmental degradation, fish farming can be a critical way to add to the global diet. Below are some of the innovations that have led Halweil to conclude that, properly guided, the explosive growth in fish farming may in fact be the most hopeful trend in the world food system.

Ecological Aquaculture

Ecological aquaculture, or "integrated multitrophic aquaculture," involves designing farms to function more like healthy aquatic ecosystems. Generally, fish farms produce waste and pollute surrounding waters because of the high concentration and limited mobility of the fish. These factors also leave the fish more susceptible to disease. However, farms that integrate complementary species can greatly reduce pollution and disease levels. Cooke Aquaculture's salmon farm in Back Bay, Canada, takes advantage of a natural ecosystem cleansing service provided by blue mussels and kelp. The shellfish filter excess waste from the fish cages, while the seaweed thrives on dissolved nutrients in the water.

Farming in the Warehouse

At the Center for Marine Biotechnology in Baltimore, Maryland, researchers are using city-supplied water and a complex filtration system to raise a few hundred fish completely indoors. Raising fish in a closed pen, either in a warehouse or floating on the ocean, avoids the common pitfalls of modern fish farming: net pens pollute coastal environments with waste and antibiotics, fish escapes threaten the diversity of wild populations, and diseases can spread easily. The Center's operation is the first indoor marine aquaculture system that can recirculate nearly all of its water and expel zero waste.

Cleaning Wastewater

If managed correctly, fish farms can go beyond addressing the problems caused by the industry itself and provide a net positive impact on the environment. Traditional ponds outside of Calcutta, India, called *bheris*, produce some 13,000 tons of fish a year for the city's 12 million inhabitants, and serve as critical bird habitat. But the bigger environmental service they provide is that the fish feed on the 600 million liters of raw sewage that spews from Calcutta daily, turning a health risk into a key urban crop.

Restoring Habitats

Fish farming can help to restore degraded coral reefs and wetlands. The metal cages that hold farmed shellfish often function as artificial reefs around which striped bass, shad, and other marine species congregate. In the Caribbean, the Caicos Conch Farm raises King conch not just to sell to restaurants around the world, but to help re-seed coral reefs with this keystone species.

Eating Local Seafood

People who eat from their local waters have a natural reason to be concerned about what goes into them. The Southold Program in Aquaculture Training (SPAT) on Long Island, New York, helps volunteers raise baby shellfish in floating cages to restore the local scallop economy. Participants receive training in algae growth, marine ecology, and shellfish dynamics, and also get to eat half their harvest of fresh, mature shellfish. In turn, they report changing their daily habits that affect water quality, such as shunning chemical fertilizers, upgrading home septic systems, and using nontoxic paint on their boats.

Eating Little Fish to Save Big Ones

In Peru, massive schools of the tiny Peruvian anchovy are netted each year. Although the fish is chock-full of the same beneficial fatty acids that have made tuna, salmon, and other big fish famous for warding off heart disease and boosting brain development, nearly all of the anchovy catch is turned into fishmeal and fish oil, used to fatten pigs and chickens on factory farms worldwide. To address this problem, students at the University of Lima have launched a campaign to change the image of the anchoveta from something that only poor people eat into a tasty dish for well-heeled sophisticates.

Factory Farming Is Not the Only Way to Feed the World

Tom Philpott

Tom Philpott was a senior food writer at Grist, an environmental news and commentary website, until May 2011, after which he began writing for Mother Jones, a progressive magazine.

To "feed the world" by 2050, we'll need a massive, global ramp-up of industrial-scale, corporate-led agriculture. At least that's the conventional wisdom.

Even progressive journalists trumpet the idea. The public-radio show *Marketplace* reported it as fact last week [in May 2011], earning a knuckle rap from [food writer] Tom Laskawy. At least one major strain of President [Barack] Obama's (rather inconsistent) agricultural policy is predicated on it. And surely most agricultural scientists and development specialists toe that line . . . right?

Well, not really. Back in 2009, *Seed Magazine* organized a forum predicated on the idea that a "scientific consensus," analogous to the one on climate change, had formed around the desirability of patent-protected genetically modified seeds. If I must say so, my own contribution to that discussion shredded that notion. If anything, a pro-GMO [genetically modified organisms] consensus has formed among a narrow group of microbiologists—the people who conduct gene manipulations to develop novel crops. But no such accord exists among scientists whose work takes them out of the laboratory and into farm fields and ecosystems: soil experts, ecologists, development specialists, etc.

Evidence Against Big Ag

The latest evidence against any consensus around Big Ag as world savior: In a paper just published in *Science*, a team of researchers led by the eminent Washington State University soil scientist John P. Reganold urges a fundamental rethinking of the U.S. ag-research system, which is "narrowly focused on productivity and efficiency" at the expense of public health and ecological resilience; and of the Farm Bill, which uses subsidies not to support a broad range of farmers but rather to "mask market, social, and environmental factors associated with conventional production systems."

The case for Big Ag had been way overblown.

The Reganold team's *Science* article distills their much longer report published last year by the prestigious National Research Council. While conventional wisdom holds that scientists who study agriculture think only lots of GMOs and agrichemicals can feed us going forward, Reganold's team has quite a different set of recommendations in mind: "organic farming, alternative livestock production (e.g., grass-fed), mixed crop and livestock systems, and perennial grains."

They are by no means the only high-level researchers to reach such conclusions. Earlier this year, the U.N.'s [United Nations] special rapporteur on food, Olivier De Schutter, conducted "an extensive review of the recent scientific literature" and concluded that the case for Big Ag had been way overblown. Defying agrichemical industry dogma about how organic agriculture produces low yields, De Schutter declared, "Small-scale farmers can double food production within 10 years in critical regions by using ecological methods."

Also this spring, another branch of the United Nations, the U.N. Environment Program, released yet another report making the case for organic and other low-input ag techniques.

And as far back as 2008, the largest-ever assessment of attitudes within the scientific community came out squarely against industrial agriculture as the true and only way to "feed the world" going forward. The International Assessment of Agricultural Knowledge, Science, and Technology for Development (IAASTD), a three-year study released in 2008, engaged 400 scientists from around the globe under the aegis of the World Bank and the U.N.'s Food and Agriculture Organization. Far from pinning hopes for humanity's future on the products of a few agrichemical firms, the IAASTD focuses on building resilience and health in communities through sustainable-ag techniques it groups under the rubric of the term "agroecology."

Now, I would never insist that there is a consensus among scientists that only organic ag can feed the world. There are clearly scientists, not all of them linked financially to the agrichemical industry, who would passionately argue against that proposition. But there is by no means a consensus in the other direction. What we have is a *debate*—one being snuffed out by the illusion of a consensus. As global population grows and climate change proceeds apace, making agriculture ever more tricky, food policy may well emerge as *the* question of our time. It's time to air out that debate.

Factory Farming Is Not Cheap, Efficient, or Healthy

Rodale Institute

Rodale Institute is a nonprofit research and policy organization that advocates for policies that support organic farming and organic farmers.

CAFO: The Tragedy of Industrial Animal Factories, edited by Daniel Imhoff and published by Watershed Media and the Foundation for Deep Ecology, is a must-read and must-see book about the horrors of Concentrated Animal Feeding Operations [CAFOs]. With over 400 photos and 30 essays, the book includes contributions from Wendell Berry, Wenonah Hauter, Fred Kirschenmann, Anna Lappé, Michael Pollan and Eric Schlosser. *CAFO* pulls back the curtain on what goes on inside so-called "factory farms" and what the effects of industrial meat production are on the animals, our environment, our communities, our agricultural system and our health. Below is a brief excerpt from the book.

Lie #1: Industrial Food Is Cheap

The retail prices of industrial meat, dairy, and egg products omit immense impacts on human health, the environment, and other shared public assets. These costs, known among economists as "externalities," include massive waste emissions with the potential to heat up the atmosphere, foul fisheries, pollute drinking water, spread disease, contaminate soils, and damage recreational areas. Citizens ultimately foot the bill with hundreds of billions of dollars in taxpayer subsidies,

Daniel Imhoff, ed., "Three Big Factory Farm Lies," in *CAFO: The Tragedy of Industrial Animal Factories*. Watershed Media, August 2010. Copyright © by Watershed Media. All rights reserved. Reproduced by permission.

medical expenses, insurance premiums, declining property values, and mounting cleanup costs.

Walk into any fast-food chain and you're likely to find a "value" meal: chicken nuggets or a cheeseburger and fries for a price almost too good to be true. For families struggling to make ends meet, a cheap meal may seem too tough to pass up. Indeed, animal factory farm promoters often point to America's bargain fast-food prices as proof that the system is working. The CAFO system, they argue, supplies affordable food to the masses. But this myth of cheap meat, dairy, and egg products revolves around mounting externalized social and ecological costs that never appear on restaurant receipts or grocery bills.

Industrial animal production brings profound health risks and costs to farmers, workers, and consumers.

Staggering Environmental Burdens

Environmental damages alone should put to rest any illusions that food produced in industrial animal factories is cheap. Soil and water have been poisoned through decades of applying synthetic fertilizers and pesticides to grow billions of tons of livestock feed. Water bodies have been contaminated with animal wastes. The atmosphere is filled with potent greenhouse gases such as carbon dioxide, methane and nitrous oxide. The mitigation costs for these problems are enormous. But what is worse, this essential cleanup work of contaminated resources is, for the most part, not being done.

To cite just one example, agricultural runoff—particularly nitrogen and phosphorus from poultry and hog farms—is a major source of pollution in the Chesapeake Bay, a once-vital East Coast fishery, now with numerous species on the verge of collapse. One study estimated the price tag for restoring the bay at $19 billion, of which $11 billion would go toward "nutrient reduction." There are over 400 such dead zones throughout the world.

Health Costs

Industrial animal production brings profound health risks and costs to farmers, workers, and consumers. CAFO workers suffer from emissions associated with industrial farming, as do neighboring communities. Medical researchers have linked the country's intensive meat consumption to such serious human health maladies as heart disease, stroke, diabetes, and certain types of cancer. Annual costs for just these diseases in the United States alone exceed $33 billion. Antibiotic-resistant organisms ("superbugs") created by overuse of antibiotics in industrial meat and dairy production can increase human vulnerability to infection. One widely cited U.S. study estimated the total annual costs of antibiotic resistance at $30 billion. Estimated U.S. annual costs associated with E. coli O157:H7, a bacteria derived primarily from animal manure, reach $405 million: $370 million for deaths, $30 million for medical care, and $5 million for lost productivity.

All these associated health problems drive up the costs of social services and insurance premiums. They reduce productivity and increase employee sick days. They can also result in premature deaths, with incalculable costs for families and communities.

Farm Communities

The retail prices of cheap animal food products also fail to reflect industrial agriculture's ongoing dislocation of farm families and the steady shuttering of businesses in rural communities. According to Robert F. Kennedy Jr., the average industrial hog factory puts ten family farmers out of business, replacing high quality agricultural jobs with three to four hourly wage workers in relatively low-paying and potentially dangerous jobs. When small farmers fall on hard times, many local employers close their doors and, at worst, entire communities, towns, and regional food production and distribution webs disappear from the landscape.

Government Subsidies

Perverse government subsidies—both in the United States and Europe—provide billions of tax dollars to support industrial animal agriculture. Tufts University researchers estimate that in the United States alone, between 1997 and 2005 the industrial animal sector saved over $35 billion as a result of federal farm subsidies that lowered the price of the feed they purchased.

Similar savings were not available to many small and midsize farmers who were growing their own feed and raising livestock in diversified pasture-based systems. Throughout the 2002 U.S. farm bill, individual CAFO investors were also eligible to receive up to $450,000 for a five-year EQIP [Environmental Quality Incentives Program] contract from the U.S. government to deal with animal wastes—allowing large operations with many investors to rake in a much greater sum. European Union agricultural subsidies also bolster industrial animal producers, providing $2.25 per dairy cow per day—25 cents more than what half the world's human population survives on.

A Less Costly Alternative

By contrast, many sustainable livestock operations address potential negative health and environmental impacts through their production methods. They produce less waste and forgo dangerous chemicals and other additives. Grass-pastured meat and dairy products have been shown to be high in omega-3 and other fatty acids that have cancer-fighting properties. Smaller farms also receive fewer and smaller federal subsidies. While sustainably produced foods may cost a bit more, many of their potential beneficial environmental and social impacts are already included in the price.

Lie #2: Industrial Food Is Efficient

Industrial food animal producers often proclaim that "bigger is better," ridiculing the "inefficiency" of small- or medium-size farms using low-impact technologies. CAFO operations, however, currently rely on heavily subsidized agriculture to produce feed, large infusions of capital to dominate markets, and lax enforcement of regulations to deal with waste disposal. Perverse incentives and market controls leverage an unfair competitive advantage over smaller producers and cloud a more holistic view of efficiency.

The efficiency of slaughterhouse practices should also be called into question.

Factory farms and CAFOs appear efficient only if we focus on the quantity of meat, milk, or eggs produced from each animal over a given period of time. But high productivity or domination of market share should not be confused with efficiency. When we measure the total cost per unit of production, or even the net profit per animal, a more sobering picture emerges. Confinement operations come with a heavy toll of external costs—inefficiencies that extend beyond the CAFO or feedlot. These hidden costs include subsidized grain discounts, unhealthy market control, depleted aquifers, polluted air and waterways, and concentrated surpluses of toxic feces and urine. The massive global acreage of monocrops that produce the corn, soybeans, and hay to feed livestock in confinement could arguably be more efficiently managed as smaller, diversified farms and pasture operations, along with protected wildlands.

Reverse Protein Factories

Animal factory farms achieve their efficiencies by substituting corn and soybeans and even wild fish for pasture grazing. To gain a pound of body weight, a broiler chicken must eat an average of 2.3 pounds of feed. Hogs convert 5.9 pounds

43

of feed into a pound of pork. Cattle require 13 pounds of feed per pound of beef, though some estimates range much higher. To supplement that feed, one-third of the world's ocean fish catch is ground up and added to rations for hogs, broiler chickens, and farmed fish. The 2006 United Nations Food and Agriculture Organization report "Livestock's Long Shadow" summed it up this way: "In simple numeric terms, livestock actually detract more from total food supply than they provide. . . . In fact, livestock consume 77 million tons of protein contained in feedstuff that could potentially be used for human nutrition, whereas 58 million tons of protein are contained in food products that livestock supply."

Total Recall

The efficiency of slaughterhouse practices should also be called into question, as their incessant increases in speed, drive for profit, and huge scale have resulted in contamination and massive meat recalls. In the United States, between spring 2007 and spring 2009 alone, there were 25 recalls due to the virulent E. coli O157:H7 pathogen involving 44 million pounds of beef. When all costs of research, prevention, and market losses are added up, over the last decade E. coli contamination has cost the beef industry an estimated $1.9 billion.

Mounting Waste

The U.S. Department of Agriculture estimates that factory animal farms generate more than 500 million tons of waste per year—more than three times the amount produced by the country's human population.

On a small, diversified farm, much of this manure could be efficiently used for fertilizer. Instead, most CAFOs store waste in massive lagoons or dry waste piles with the potential to give off toxic fumes, leak, or overflow. Ground and surface water can be contaminated with bacteria and antibiotics; pesticides and hormones containing endocrine disruptors; or dangerously high levels of nitrogen, phosphorus, and other nutrients. Inconsistent enforcement of regulations has allowed CAFO waste disposal problems to escalate in many areas.

Meanwhile, the environmental and health impacts of this pollution are rarely calculated as part of the narrow range of parameters that CAFO operators use to define efficiency.

Another issue clouding any meaningful discussions of efficiency is the lack of access to markets among many independent producers.

Government Subsidies

Not only do CAFOs burden citizens with environmental and health costs, they also gorge themselves at the proverbial public trough. Thanks to U.S. government subsidies, between 1997 and 2005, factory farms saved an estimated $3.9 billion per year because they were able to purchase corn and soybeans at prices below what it cost to grow the crops.

Without these feed discounts, amounting to a 5 to 15 percent reduction in operating costs, it is unlikely that many of these industrial factory farms could remain profitable. By contrast, many small farms that produce much of their own forage receive no government money. Yet they are expected somehow to match the efficiency claims of the large, subsidized megafactory farms. On this uneven playing field, CAFOs may falsely appear to "outcompete" their smaller, diversified counterparts.

Anticompetitiveness

Another issue clouding any meaningful discussions of efficiency is the lack of access to markets among many independent producers. Because CAFOs have direct relationships with meat packers (and are sometimes owned by them, or "vertically integrated"), they have preferred access to the decreasing number of slaughterhouses and distribution channels to process and market products. Many midsize or smaller independent producers have no such access and as a result must get big, develop separate distribution channels, or simply disappear.

Lie #3: Industrial Food Is Healthy

Industrial animal food production heightens the risk of the spread of food-borne illnesses that afflict millions of Americans each year. Rates of heart disease, cancer, diabetes, and obesity—often related to excessive meat and dairy consumption—are at an all-time high. Respiratory diseases and outbreaks of illnesses are increasingly common among CAFO and slaughterhouse workers and spill over into neighboring communities and the public at large.

The Centers for Disease Control and Prevention (CDC) estimate that contaminated meat- and poultry-related infections make up to 3 million people sick each year, killing at least 1,000—figures that are probably underreported.

Crammed into tight confinement areas in massive numbers, factory farm animals often become caked with their own feces. Animal waste is the primary source of infectious bacteria such as E. coli and Salmonella, which affect human populations through contaminated food and water. Grain-intensive diets can also increase the bacterial and viral loads in confined animal wastes. As a result, CAFOs can become breeding grounds for diseases and pathogens.

Dietary Impacts

Americans consume more meat and poultry per capita today than ever before, part of a diet that is high in calories and rich in saturated fats. According to the Center for a Livable Future at Johns Hopkins University, meat and dairy foods contribute all of the cholesterol and are the primary source of saturated fat in the typical American diet. Approximately two-thirds of Americans are overweight or obese, increasing their chances of developing breast, colon, pancreas, kidney, and other cancers. Obesity and high blood cholesterol levels are among the leading risk factors for heart disease. Both of these conditions are associated with heavy meat consumption. More directly, researchers have linked diets that include significant amounts of animal fat to an increased incidence of cardiovascular disease.

On the other hand, studies regularly show that vegetarians exhibit the lowest incidence of heart problems. High intakes of fruits, vegetables, whole grains and Mediterranean dietary patterns (rich in plant-based foods and unsaturated fats) have been shown to reduce the incidence of chronic diseases and associated risk factors, including body mass index and obesity.

Contaminated Feed

Animal feeding practices also raise important health concerns. Corn and soybeans, for example, have been shown to absorb dioxins, PCBs, and other potential human carcinogens through air pollution. Once fed to animals, these persistent compounds can be stored in animal fat reserves. These harmful pollutants can later move up the food chain when animal fats left over from slaughter are rendered and used again for animal feed. As fats are recycled in the animal feeding system, the result is a higher concentration of dioxins and PCBs in the animal fats consumed by people. Animal and plant fats, both of which can store dioxins and PCBs, can compose up to 8 percent of animal feed rations.

Worker Health

CAFO workers suffer from numerous medical conditions, including repetitive motion injuries and respiratory illness associated with poor air quality. Studies indicate that at least 25 percent of CAFO workers experience respiratory diseases such as chronic bronchitis and occupational asthma.

Slaughterhouse workers are also at risk for work-related health conditions. In early 2008, for example, an unknown neurological illness began afflicting employees at a factory run by Quality Pork Processors in Minnesota, which slaughters 1,900 pigs a day. The diseased workers suffered burning sensations and numbness as well as weakness in the arms and legs. All the victims worked at or near the "head table," using compressed air to dislodge pigs' brains from their skulls. Inhalation of microscopic pieces of pig brain is suspected to have caused the illness. After a CDC investigation, this practice was discontinued.

Community Health

CAFOs can put neighboring communities at risk of exposure to dangerous air and water contaminants. More than a million Americans, for example, take drinking water from groundwater contaminated by nitrogen-containing pollutants, mostly derived from agricultural fertilizers and animal waste applications. Several studies have linked nitrates in the drinking water to birth defects, disruption of thyroid function, and various types of cancers. Further, the use of antibiotics on livestock over sustained periods is widely acknowledged to increase the prevalence of antibiotic-resistant bacteria.

Infections from these new "superbugs" are difficult to treat and increase human risk of disease. In a study of 226 North Carolina schools, children living within three miles of factory farms had significantly higher asthma rates and more asthma-related emergency room visits than children living more than three miles away. A separate study found that people living close to intensive swine operations suffer more negative mood states (e.g., tension, depression, anger, reduced vigor, fatigue, and confusion) than control groups. Exposure to hydrogen sulfide—given off by concentrated animal feeding operations—has been linked to neuropsychiatric abnormalities.

Food production that is safe for the environment, humane to animals, and sound for workers and communities gives us the best chance for a food system that is safe and healthy for eaters and producers alike.

Small Diversified Farming Systems Will Be Crucial to the Future of Global Food Production

Eileen Ecklund

Eileen Ecklund is a writer and editor from the San Francisco area.

When American families sit down to dinner, often the concern is to avoid eating too much. Yet in 2010, the United Nations' [UN] Food and Agriculture Organization (FAO) estimated that more than 900 million people around the world were undernourished. By 2050, the world's population is projected to rise to somewhere around 9 billion—and more people will likely be eating more meat, which takes more resources and energy to produce than most crops.

How on earth will our agricultural systems feed all those mouths, especially while coping with climate change, soil degradation and erosion, water shortages, and rising energy prices? And can it be done without increasing the environmental damage attributed to industrial farming practices?

Maybe, if we can learn to see landscapes through the eyes of a bee. That may seem a tall order for such a tiny insect, but Claire Kremen believes that understanding what is good for bees is a first step toward shaping agricultural ecosystems, or "agroecosystems," that can sustain both humans and natural biodiversity, without the need for the huge inputs of chemicals and energy that have made industrial farming practices so damaging. Kremen, a conservation biologist and professor in the Department of Environmental Science, Policy, and Management (ESPM) [at University of California, Berkeley], was studying the effects of natural habitat on the crop pollination services of wild bees when she made an observation that would alter the focus of her research. The farms in her study that were more biodiverse, growing multiple crops with organic techniques, interspersed with natural habitat, seemed able to "grow their own bees," providing sufficient food and nesting resources to act as oases for wild pollinators in the midst of otherwise intensively farmed landscapes. These farms could rely to a large degree on wild bees to pollinate their crops, while farms growing only one crop had to import European honeybees for pollination.

A 2008 report . . . concluded that modern agriculture would have to shift rapidly away from industrialized systems and toward sustainable, small-scale, diversified farming systems.

This discovery put Kremen on the road to realizing that most or even all of the inputs that modern commercial farms require—chemical pesticides and fertilizers, wasteful amounts of water and energy, imported pollinators—were needed only because the monoculture-dominated landscapes created by industrial agriculture lacked biodiversity.

"From studying the pollinators, I realized that the way we conduct agriculture has basically required us to replace all of the ecosystem services that used to be in the agricultural ecosystem with substitutes," she says. If farmers could bring back many of the traditional practices that supported biodiversity, enhanced by the application of modern ecological science, Kremen believes that the world could produce more food while reducing agriculture's harmful effects, making it more sustainable over the long term.

Support for Small-Scale Agriculture

A growing number of policy-makers and researchers are thinking along the same lines. A 2008 report released by the International Assessment of Agricultural Science and Technology for Development, a multinational effort spearheaded by the World Bank and the FAO, concluded that modern agriculture would have to shift rapidly away from industrialized systems and toward sustainable, small-scale, diversified farming systems in order to meet the challenges of population growth, hunger, environmental degradation, and climate change.

And in March of this year [2011], the UN Special Rapporteur on the Right to Food, Olivier De Schutter, issued a report asserting that small-scale farmers in the poorest regions could double their food production within 10 years by applying agroecological principles. He made this assertion based on the work of a number of agroecological researchers, including ESPM professor Miguel Altieri, and cited as evidence several recent studies of sustainable agriculture projects in poor countries that found substantial increases in crop yields—in some cases more than double—as well as improvements in the farms' environmental services. De Schutter urged countries and philanthropic groups to invest in research and adopt policies to help scale up agroecological practices.

Kremen and a group of UC [University of California] Berkeley colleagues from a variety of disciplines are leading the charge, establishing a new Berkeley Center for Diversified Farming Systems to bring together researchers, writers, and practitioners from many fields to focus on feeding the world's growing population through diversified, multifunctional agriculture that also addresses the poverty and lack of access to land that are the root causes of hunger. The Berkeley Institute of the Environment has already hosted a series of roundtables and presentations on topics related to diversified farming systems, with more to come.

In addition to Kremen, affiliated faculty include Altieri, Lynn Huntsinger, Nathan Sayre, Alastair Iles, Christy Getz, David Zilberman, and Justin Brashares.

These practices . . . help to build healthy, productive soil and reduce water use.

Berkeley is uniquely positioned to host this interdisciplinary research and education center, Kremen says, because of its world-renowned faculty in the fields of agroecology, science, technology, society, agricultural economics, and rural sociology. Notes [Lynn] Huntsinger: "That's the beauty of our college, that we can bring all these things together."

Promoting Biodiversity Across Scales

Generally speaking, a diversified farming system is one that promotes biodiversity across spatial scales, from plot to field to landscape. Crops are planted and livestock raised in combination, resulting in interactions that sponsor the functioning of the farming systems in ways that replenish natural ecosystems. Methods employed within a diversified farm may include minimal soil tillage, growing multiple crops together, planting cover crops, and interspersing trees and shrubs with crops and livestock.

These practices also provide pollination, pest and disease control, water purification, and erosion control. They help to build healthy, productive soil and reduce water use, as demonstrated by research conducted in both the Altieri and Kremen labs on farms in Napa, Sonoma, and Yolo counties [in California].

"Diversified farming systems produce and regenerate the ecosystem services that the agricultural system needs," Kremen says. This allows farmers to forgo the harmful inputs and practices required in industrial farming, which is beneficial for the biodiversity that in turn produces the services. "I see it as a cycle."

At the landscape scale, diversified farming practices include coordination among land managers to protect wildlands in and around agricultural areas, and the support of ecological practices on rangelands and in forests. "In California, 35 million acres of rangelands are providing all kinds of services, from habitat for pollinators to livestock products to viewsheds," says Huntsinger, a range ecologist and manager.

Some heritage systems, like the Ifugao rice terraces of the Philippines, maximize the use of mountainous terrain for rice production while incorporating stands of managed forest and a variety of aquatic and terrestrial wildlife. Other systems combine traditional farming techniques with modern ecological science and innovative marketing and distribution methods; Kremen points to Full Belly Farm in California's Capay Valley, which successfully raises more than 80 different crops, wresting a huge amount of produce from a small area. Even industrial farms can become more biodiverse through the application of improved techniques. Monocrops such as vineyards, for example, can be broken up with flowering cover crops, hedgerows, and corridors that help control pests without chemical inputs.

How to Feed Nine Billion?

For all their potential benefits, the question remains: Can diversified farming systems feed a growing, changing world? Perhaps a better question might be, can we feed the world without them? Despite the tremendous crop yields made possible by industrial farming and the technologies of the Green Revolution of the 1960s and '70s, 900 million people still do not get enough to eat, and starvation has become a recurrent feature of life in sub-Saharan Africa. Increasing the food supply is not enough; that food needs to get to those who can least afford it.

"The Green Revolution didn't solve world hunger; it solved the number of calories," Kremen says.

The solution lies in supporting small-scale farmers.

Most of the food consumed in developing nations is produced by small farmers, many of them still using subsistence methods. Their farms are where the productivity gains must come from, and the question, Kremen says, is whether countries will adopt policies that favor industrial intensification, or sustainable intensification based on agroecological principles.

One of the key reasons that the Green Revolution bypassed the world's poorest farmers is that they couldn't afford its technologies. In his report to the UN, De Schutter pointed to evidence that agroecological methods outperform chemical fertilizers in boosting the amount of food produced by subsistence farmers. Many of these methods are inexpensive but require more labor—which could create more rural jobs and help to alleviate poverty.

"We won't solve hunger and stop climate change with industrial farming on large plantations," De Schutter said in a statement accompanying the report's release. "The solution lies in supporting small-scale farmers' knowledge and experimentation, and in raising incomes of smallholders so as to contribute to rural development."

Industrial agriculture isn't likely to disappear any time soon, and many experts believe that any solution to the twinned problems of hunger and resource depletion will require some combination of industrial and sustainable methods. Some, like agricultural economist [David] Zilberman, argue that modern industrial technologies, particularly genetic engineering, could have a crucial role to play in helping agriculture to wean itself from the worst of its chemical abuses, through pest-resistant crop varieties, and to adapt to climate change by developing heat- and drought-tolerant varieties.

"Diversified farming systems are crucial to the future of the university, California, and even to global food production, but the concept really has to be inclusive of modern biotechnologies," Zilberman says. "It has to take the best of science that's sustainable and combine it with environmentalism."

Kremen says that, while the economics perspective is a key one for this growing interdisciplinary group, she is skeptical about the ultimate value of genetic engineering, arguing that genetically modified organisms are just another variety of the reductionist, high-tech approach that has led to so many of industrial agriculture's worst abuses. "People love technological fixes," she says. "But spending so much effort to produce these engineered varieties that then have severe vulnerabilities or cause new problems is not, I think, a very good strategy. I'd rather see that effort put into coming up with agroecologically designed communities that do the same thing—that use water and nutrients really efficiently."

Altieri, who calls agroecology "the antithesis of transgenic technology," says that "there is not one acre of transgenics that feeds the one billion poor people. Transgenic corn and soybean are produced to feed cattle that the poor cannot afford, and for biofuels, canola, and cotton that don't feed anybody."

Investing in Research

Creating and supporting diversified agricultural systems, both in developing and developed countries, will require a substantial investment in research, and not just in the natural sciences. Work in fields like economics, sociology, and public policy can help societies grow a sustainable, biodiverse system of food production and distribution that allows farmers to not merely survive, but thrive.

"Structurally, one of the biggest challenges to truly sustainable agriculture is the push to do everything as cheaply as possible," says Christy Getz, who studies farm labor conditions and other societal factors. "Most profits in the organic sector go to the largest players in the food chain; very few small organic farmers make significant profits. Continued industrialization, concentration, and consolidation are changing the face of organic agriculture."

Another challenge is to identify the best methods for encouraging farmers in developed countries to switch from industrial to diversified farming practices, research that [Berkeley faculty member Alastair] Iles, whose field is environmental law and policy, is pursuing. Among the questions he's investigating are: How can farmer motivations be better linked to the science of agroecology? Through setting rules, or through creating economic incentives, or by creating peer pressure? How can we evaluate the effectiveness of different types of policies?

The goal of establishing the Center for Diversified Farming Systems is to close some of these research gaps—by providing a venue where scholars can share their work, and by helping to train future leaders in the field who in turn will translate agroecological scientific advances into practice. Ultimately, the aim of Kremen and her Berkeley colleagues is to create a place where ideas about how to create a sustainable future for human agriculture can be debated, and the best winnowed from the crop.

Don't Believe the Lie: Organic Farming CAN Feed the World

Ethan A. Huff

Ethan A. Huff is the main staff writer for Natural News, an on-line environmental news website.

One of the arguments often used to defend genetically-modified (GM) crops purports that biotechnology is necessary to feed the world, as non-GM and organic farming methods by themselves are incapable of producing enough food for everyone. But the truth of the matter is that organic farming by itself is fully capable of feeding the world—we just need to make a few changes to the way we grow and raise our food, which includes putting an end to the factory farming methods that are destroying our health and the planet.

In a report entitled *Feeding the Future,* the *Soil Association,* a U.K.-based organic farming advocacy group, makes the case that organic and other agro-ecological farming systems are not only the solution to the world's hunger problems, but when implemented, these holistic methods of growing food actually facilitate bringing the world's poorest out of poverty.

On the flip side, GM farming systems perpetuate and even create poverty because they lock farmers into an endless cycle of dependence on corporations for both the next season's batch of self-destructing seeds, and the toxic chemical cock-tails required to grow them. GM agriculture, in other words, is toxic to the world's economies, toxic to human health, and toxic to the environment.

As was shown in a recent Rodale Institute study, which was the culmination of more than 30 years worth of research, organic farming systems actually produce higher yields than GM and non-GM conventional farming systems. Organic farming is also fully self-renewing and sustainable, as composting, manure, and other organic fertilizing methods naturally enrich soil and eliminate the need for toxic pesticides and herbicides (http://www.naturalnews.com/033925_organic _farming_crop_yields.html).

As much as 40 percent of the world's grains are fed to factory farm animals.

Besides the GMO issue, factory farming systems in general, including confined animal feeding operations (CAFOs), are needlessly depleting much of the world's supply of grains. According to the Soil Association, as much as 40 percent of all the world's cereals are fed to livestock, and this could rise to 50 percent by 2050 if current trends continue.

Ruminating animals like cows and sheep were meant to eat grasses on pasture, not GM soy, corn, and the many other grains that are routinely fed to them on factory farms. Besides making the animals sick, as they were not designed to eat them, these grain mixtures require an intense amount of resources to grow and produce.

By letting animals graze naturally on pasture grasses, which humans cannot eat anyway, these grains could instead be used to feed humans. And grass-fed animals produce far healthier meat than grain-fed animals anyway, which means that human health across the globe would improve dramatically just from making the switch (http://www.naturalnews.com /027199_meat_fat_cattle.html).

Particularly in the developed world, humans waste an incredible amount of food. The Soil Association says that roughly one third of all food produced for human consumption ends up getting wasted. So if more people simply made a conscious effort to conserve food, or at least come up with simple ways to share unused food with those in need, hunger in many areas of the world would subside dramatically (http://www.naturalnews.com/033885_food_waste_America.html).

One third of the world's food ends up in the trash heap as waste.

The group also mentions a type of food rationing system as another option, but such a tyrannical approach would be wholly unnecessary if the other methods were implemented, and if more people began growing their own organic food at home.

CHAPTER 2

Is Factory Farming an Ethical Way to Treat Animals?

Chapter Preface

One hotly debated issue concerning factory farming is the treatment of farm animals. Between 2000 and 2012, animal rights groups were effective in publicizing shocking examples of animal abuse at animal production companies and slaughterhouses in the United States. Often, these groups do so by posting videos obtained by animal rights activists and investigators who surreptitiously enter or work undercover at these locations in order to expose animal living conditions or slaughter practices. Factory farms and slaughterhouse operators are fighting back, however, by trying to pass laws to make it a crime to videotape farm animals or farm animal workers without the permission of the farm owner, laws that are sometimes referred to by the media as *ag gag* laws.

One example of animal rights tactics surfaced in August 2012 when the US Department of Agriculture (USDA) received a video from the animal rights group Compassion Over Killing showing workers at a California slaughterhouse engaged in a number of acts of abuse, including sending a partly stunned and still conscious cow to slaughter by lifting it in the air by one leg. The plant supplies meat not only to the USDA school lunch program but also to Costco and fast food chains such as McDonald's. The government shut down the plant in response to the video but allowed it to reopen a few days later. Similar videos can be found on the websites of many local and national animal rights groups and are often released to the media. Besides shocking incidents of cruelty by workers against farm animals similar to the recent California story, these videos typically expose the day-to-day living conditions of farm animals. Examples include chickens crammed so tightly into indoor cages that they can barely turn around and pigs housed in indoor metal gestation crates hardly bigger than they are, conditions that activists say cause the animals stress and suffering. For most Americans, who know little about how their food is really produced, the videos provide graphic evidence of the fate of farm animals in the modern food production system. Animal rights groups use the videos to drive public opinion and put pressure on food producers to change their policies and provide better treatment for animals.

Ag gag laws aim to stop this kind of negative publicity. The nation's first ag gag laws were passed in the early 1990s in the farm states of North Dakota, Montana, and Kansas. Largely in order to silence animal rights whistleblowers, a number of other states subsequently introduced this type of legislation into their legislatures, including Florida, Iowa, Minnesota, and New York, all of which considered but failed to pass such bills in 2011. In 2012, however, Utah and Iowa were successful in passing ag gag laws. Thus, five states had made undercover work by animal welfare groups illegal, and by mid-2012 similar legislation was pending in several other states, including Minnesota, Missouri, Nebraska, and Tennessee. In the states with ag gag laws, provisions and penalties sometimes differ. In North Dakota, for example, it is a Class B misdemeanor subject to a thirty-day jail sentence to enter an animal facility and use a camera, video recorder, or any other type of video or audio recording device. Other state laws have a different approach with harsher penalties. For example, Iowa makes it a crime to obtain employment under false pretenses and imposes a jail sentence of up to two years for doing so.

Critics of the ag gag laws question whether these laws are constitutional, given that they seem to restrict First Amendment press and speech freedoms and are designed to limit public awareness and debate about animal conditions that may be unsanitary, unhealthy, and unethical. In some cases, producers who have been revealed as abusers have also had problems with product recalls due to unsafe products such as eggs or meat. The ag gag laws, therefore, could cover up the use of dying or sick animals or other unsafe practices that may infect the food supply. Activists maintain that the government does not effectively regulate or investigate food producers and that the ag gag laws protect a food system that is unsafe and rife with animal suffering and terrible working conditions for animal workers.

The issues of whether conditions can be improved for animals at factory farms and whether the industrial production of animal-based food products is inherently abusive are the subject of viewpoints included in this chapter. Authors of these viewpoints debate the basic question of whether factory farming is an ethical way to treat farm animals.

Most Factory Farms Use Healthy and Responsible Animal Practices

Katerina Athanasiou

Katerina Athanasiou is a student of urban and regional studies at Cornell University. Her particular interest is sustainable transportation and food systems.

From *Food, Inc.* to Michael Pollan's novels, in recent years, the public at large has criticized agriculture. Often, the public portrays farmers as villains. Busy farmers frequently remain unheard in the media. Recently, ABC ran a special with the headline, "Got Milk? Got Ethics? Animal Rights v. U.S. Dairy Industry."

This upset students from farming backgrounds, like Kelly Lee '13 from Mill Wheel Farm in Johnson Creek, Wisconsin. She said, "I was really upset that was the portrayal of the dairy industry. That was one farm in one instance, where things weren't up to standard. Most farms in the US use healthy and responsible management practices."

Misperceptions About Factory Farms

Prof. Michael Van Amburgh, animal science, is advisor of the Cornell University Dairy Science Club (CUDS). He suggested that many of the negative perceptions of dairy farmers emerge due to public opinion of animal welfare.

He believes that public view of animal treatment is caused by "anthropomorphism," or the allocation of human qualities to animals. For example, animal images infiltrate popular culture through the personification of animals in books and cartoons. From these sources, the public generates the notion that animals have needs that parallel those of humans.

Concentrated Animal Feeding Operations (CAFO) are farms that raise animals in confined area while adhering to the Environmental Protection Agency's (EPA) criteria. Consequently, they carry a negative connotation.

Van Amburgh stressed that "animals want routine," and explained that accommodations within farms, like sprinklers and fans, allow for optimal living conditions.

Some believe tight living conditions produce unhappy and unhealthy animals. In the state of New York, any Animal Feeding Operation with over 200 animals is considered a CAFO, and therefore, must conform to strict regulations.

Van Amburgh shared a story from another state, where regulations restricted a farmer with a 4,300-cow farm. When his municipality approached him about dumping waste on his property, he refused. Because EPA regulations apply only to larger farms, the municipality approached a 100-cow farm, where such parameters do not exist. The smaller farm allowed the municipality to dump there.

This story does not imply the small farm size alleviates farmers of responsibility. Instead, it indicates that the stricter guidelines for larger farms serve to monitor situations.

In a yet unpublished study conducted in Vancouver, cows were given the choice to either graze in open pastures or stay in closed barns. Overwhelmingly, the cows chose to stay within the barn, only selecting to go outdoors in the evenings after sunset. Van Amburgh stressed that "animals want routine," and explained that accommodations within farms, like sprinklers and fans, allow for optimal living conditions.

CUDS President, Sam Fesseden '11 said, "If a farm is trying to make profit, they need to have animals producing a good amount of product. In order to produce, you must have healthy, happy animals. If we were farming sick animals, then we wouldn't be making profit."

Many CUDS members took offense to the term "factory farm" and its negative connotations, pointing out that farmers are simply trying to make a living for themselves. Farmers cannot simply sacrifice the health of their animals without risking their own wellbeing.

In the article, "Demystifying the Environmental Sustainability of Food Production" Prof. Jude Capper, dairy sciences, Washington State University, with Cornell colleagues noted that cow feed would be considered waste products from human food, fiber and biofuel production.

The environmental impacts of farms generate further criticism. In terms of efficiency, although the average dairy cow produces 27.8 kilograms of carbon dioxide equivalents compared to 13.5 kilograms of carbon dioxide equivalents in 1944, the carbon dioxide equivalents produced per kilogram of milk have decreased from 3.66 to 1.35 according to Capper's article.

Consumers Disconnected from Farming

Some miscommunication between farmers and the public results from the disconnect between the general public and any form of agriculture.

According to the U.S. Census Bureau, 80 percent of U.S. citizens reside in metropolitan settings. In a census of the EPA, less than 1 percent of the population claimed occupational farming.

Animal Science PhD candidate, Rick Watters, grad, suggested that, because so many Americans live away from farming, they rely on past views of farming. Van Amburgh described his grandfather's 100-acre farm with 10 to 20 cows; without his direct experience with farming, Van Amburgh believes this might be his view of agriculture.

Van Amburgh said, "They [media against dairy farming] are being produced by well funded groups with an agenda."

Farmers often lack the time and resources to fund their own media, which could potentially depict their own image.

Prof. Gary Fick, crop and soil sciences, said, "It's difficult to dictate right and wrong when dairy farming, taking another animal's milk, is such an unnatural process to begin with."

This relationship between agriculture and milk (a natural, nutrient-rich substance) arouses questions of morality. Certain farming practices, despite their appearance, may be necessary.

For example, ABC's "Got Milk? Got Ethics? Animal Rights v. U.S. Dairy Industry" showed a clip of "docking." "Docking" is a procedure that removes a cow's tail. Though the practice may appear gruesome, to some, it is typically performed.

According to Lee, docking improves worker hygiene, effectively controls disease transmission and increases comfort during milking.

CUDS member Lauren Osborn '13 explained, "People don't understand the necessity of these practices."

The Pork Industry Is Committed to Responsible Animal Care

National Pork Board

The National Pork Board was created by Congress and charged with providing consumer information, conducting research, and promoting pork as an agricultural product.

The National Pork Board disagrees with the portrayal of pork production shown in a video produced by Mercy for Animals and released on Wednesday [July 18, 2012].

Pig Farmers Care About Pig Welfare

The National Pork Board and the pig farmers of America have a deep commitment and responsibility to the welfare of the animals we raise. "Pig farmers have a strong track record of animal husbandry practices that have been developed with the help of research on what is best for the animal. And as an industry, we are always seeking to improve those practices," said Conley Nelson, a farmer and pig-production executive from Algona, Iowa, who also is president of the National Pork Board. "Christensen Farms has always exemplified that commitment and we support their efforts to further investigate this video to ensure the farm's employees and practices remain at the standards we all expect."

An independent panel of scientists and ethicists who reviewed the video concluded there were no signs of animal abuse or neglect.

"Raising animals for food is not an easy job, but it's one we are passionate about. It is also complicated," Conley said.

"Rather than basing judgments on a grainy, heavily edited video, we urge consumers to seek out more information. For example, many of the practices shown in this latest hidden camera video are described in great detail in two videos on our website, *A Good End for Pigs* and *Castration and Tail Docking of Piglets*."

"Animal care can be a personal and emotional issue for many consumers—particularly when presented through a video that is designed to stimulate a negative reaction. The way that we raise pigs today, however, has evolved as we've worked to improve food safety, environmental protection, and animal care. These principles should continue to guide any decision made about the best way to care for our animals."

"While top veterinary experts confirm that the methods we use today are scientifically sound and humane, we know that we must continue working to improve the way that we raise and care for our animals. We have invested millions of farmer checkoff dollars into improving animal welfare—including evaluating new sow housing options and more humane methods of euthanasia. We urge those companies and organizations that care about improving animal welfare to join us in this important initiative."

The National Pork Board has responsibility for Checkoff-funded research, promotion and consumer information projects and for communicating with pork producers and the public. Through a legislative national Pork Checkoff, pork producers invest $0.40 for each $100 value of hogs sold. Importers of pork products contribute a like amount, based on a formula. The Pork Checkoff funds national and state programs in advertising, consumer information, retail and food-service marketing, export market promotion, production improvement, technology, swine health, pork safety and environmental management.

Factory Farms Produce Meat in Unethical Ways

Last Chance for Animals

Last Chance for Animals (LCA) is a national, nonprofit animal advocacy organization, which was founded by animal rights activist Chris DeRose and is dedicated to investigating, exposing, and ending animal exploitation.

Factory farming is an industrial process in which animals and the products they generate are mass produced. The animals are not seen as individual, sentient beings with unique physical and psychological needs but as eggs, milk, meat, leather etc. Because factory farming is a business, its goal is to maximize production and, consequently, profit. Since the animals are seen as mere commodities, they are bred, fed, confined, and drugged to lay more eggs, birth more offspring, and die with more meat on their bones.

Farmers cut costs by feeding animals the remains of other animals, keeping them in extremely small and soiled enclosures, and refusing to provide bedding. Because animals live in such a manner and are denied normal social interactions, they experience boredom and stress so great that it leads to unnatural aggression. To curb this aggression, conceal the disease that results from such horrendous living conditions, and stimulate aberrant growth, farmers routinely administer drugs to animals, which in turn reach meat-eating consumers. The consequences of this agribusiness are institutionalized animal cruelty, environmental destruction and resource depletion, and health dangers. . . .

Broiler Chickens

Farmers get more money for chickens with enlarged thighs and breasts. As a result, they breed the animals to be so heavy that their bones cannot support their weight. Consequently, the chickens have difficulty standing, and their legs often break. Like other factory farmed animals, broiler chickens are raised in such overcrowded enclosures that they become aggressive. To stop them from fighting with one another, their beaks and toes are cut off without anesthetic. Some cannot eat after being "debeaked" and starve. They never breathe fresh air but instead inhale ammonia day after day.

Diseases Common to Broiler Chickens

- Respiratory diseases

- Bacterial infections

- Keratoconjunctivitis

- Dehydration induced ailments

- Heart attacks

- Congestive heart failure

- Heat prostration

- Osteoporosis

- Cancer

- Crippled legs

Layer Chickens

Layer chickens lay 90–95% of the eggs sold in the U.S. Newborn chicks are placed on a conveyor belt where a worker picks each one up to see if it is male or female. Newborn males are placed in trash bags and suffocated, decapitated, gassed, crushed, or ground up alive. Newborn females are placed back on the belt. The next worker then picks up the female chick, holds her up to a machine's hot iron which cuts off her beak, and then places her back on the belt. The beaks of these birds are removed because five to eight of them are crammed into 14 square inch cages, cages so small that the birds cannot even spread their wings. Such close confinement, which averts their natural social order, causes aggression among the birds. Debeaking prevents them from harming one another, which would make their corpses less profitable to the farmers. It is a painful practice that involves slicing through bone, cartilage, and soft tissue.

The floors of layer hens' "battery cages" are made of extremely uncomfortable wire, which chafes their skin, rips out some of their feathers, bruises their bodies, and deforms their feet. The cage floor slopes at the bottom, so weaker hens are often crushed on the cage base. Layer hens' bones are so brittle that they often shatter during handling. Approximately one in five die of stress and disease. Others are ground up and turned into animal feed on site.

Forced Molting

Layer hens are exposed to light constantly so that they will lay more eggs. At the end of their laying cycle, they are killed or subjected to "forced molting," a process that entails withholding food and water for up to 18 days and keeping them in darkness so that their bodies are shocked into another laying cycle. Many of the birds who undergo forced molting die from fatigue.

Diseases Common to Layer Hens

- Cage Layer Fatigue

- Respiratory diseases

- Bacterial infections

- Fatty Liver Syndrome

- Broken bones

• Paralysis

Hens normally live 15 to 20 years. Layer hens are slaughtered when they are one to two years old.

Inside the slaughterhouse, the turkeys are hung by their feet from metal shackles on a conveyor belt.

Turkeys

Turkeys are given less than three square feet of cage space. The end of their beaks are cut off and their toes are clipped, both without anesthesia. Farmers get more money for turkeys with enlarged breasts. They thus breed the animals to be so heavy that their bones cannot support their weight. As a result, turkeys have difficulty standing and their legs often break; some are trampled underfoot. Moreover, they are so heavy that they cannot reproduce naturally. Consequently, they must be artificially inseminated.

The Slaughterhouse

Turkeys are loaded onto a conveyor belt. Some fall onto the ground instead of landing on the belt. Because workers are in such a rush, they rarely pick up those that have fallen. As a result, some birds die after being crushed by machinery operated near the unloading area. Others succumb to starvation and exposure.

Inside the slaughterhouse, the turkeys are hung by their feet from metal shackles on a conveyor belt. Their heads are dunked in the stunning tank, an electrical bath of water. Because too much electricity would damage the turkey's carcass, therein diminishing its sale value, the electrical current is often set lower than that necessary to render the birds unconscious. Thus many birds emerge from the tank still alert. The turkeys' throats are then cut. The blade misses some birds, who move on to the next assembly line station, the scalding tank, a cistern of boiling hot water. Those birds, nicknamed "redskins," are boiled alive. . . .

Cattle Raised for Beef

Range cattle are frightened and confused when humans come to round them up and pack them onto trucks; injuries often result. During transport, they are frightened, exposed to severe weather conditions, and deprived of food, water, and veterinary care. The cows are taken to auction where they are sold to the highest bidder, then returned to the range, taken directly to slaughter, or brought to a feedlot.

Cattle are then burned with a hot iron brand without anesthetic so that [it] is clear who "owns" them. Beef cattle are also subjected to "waddling," during which ranchers cut chunks out of the hide (which hangs under their neck) for identification purposes. Finally, they are castrated and dehorned without anesthetic.

Feedlots

At feedlots, beef cattle live in dusty holding pens where they are forced to eat and sleep in their own excrement. They are given growth hormones and, because the air is so full of bacteria, many contract respiratory disease.

Diseases Common to Cattle Raised for Beef

- Cancer eye

- Respiratory disease

- Metabolic disorders

The Slaughterhouse

Approximately 250 cows are killed every hour at the typical beef slaughterhouse. Because workers are in a rush to stay on schedule and kill such a large number of animals in such a short period of time, the animals are often treated rather cruelly. To accustom themselves to life at the slaughterhouse, workers must become desensitized to the animals' suffering and conceive of these sentient creatures as mere objects; this conceptualization obviously leads to inhumane treatment. Moreover, the turnover rate at slaughterhouses is so high that there are a lot of new, inexperienced technicians who cannot properly sedate cows, among other things. Although cattle are supposed to be rendered unconscious before being killed, workers frequently do not successfully "stun" the animals. As a result, conscious, struggling cows are hung upside down. Their throats are then cut.

Dairy Cows

Dairy cows live in crowded pens or barns with concrete floors. Milking machines often cut them and cause other injuries. Some give them electrical shocks which cause extreme pain and even death. Dairy cows are forced to produce 10 times more milk than they would produce in nature. As a result, they experience numerous health problems.

Diseases Common to Dairy Cows

- Mastitis, a bacterial infection of the udders

- Bovine Leukemia Virus

- Bovine Immunodeficiency

- Johne's Disease

- Milk Fever

- Metabolic disorders such as ketosis and laminitis

- Birth defects caused by Bovine Growth Hormone

- Udder ligament damage

- Drugs Given to Dairy Cows

- Bovine Growth Hormone

- Prostaglandin

- Antibiotics

- Tranquilizers

Cows normally live 20 to 25 years or more. Dairy cows are slaughtered when they are three or five years old, mostly for use in fast food hamburgers.

After being impregnated, sows are placed in 18 to 24 inch wide pens or metal gestation crates.

Dairy Calves

After dairy cows give birth, their calves are separated from them, a practice which causes cows great sadness: they can be heard bellowing for their young. They are then milked repeatedly for the fluid meant for their calf. Female dairy calves replace older dairy cows who can no longer give as much milk as farmers demand. Male calves are raised and killed for their meat, both beef and veal.

Veal Calves

Veal calves live in small wooden crates; some are chained. They cannot turn around or even stretch their legs. The floors of their stalls are slatted, causing them severe joint and leg pain. Since their mother's milk is taken for human consumption, they are fed a milk substitute deficient in iron and fiber. In other words, they are deliberately kept anemic and their muscles are atrophied so that their flesh will be pale and tender. Craving iron, they lick the metallic parts of their stalls, even those covered in urine. Water is often withheld from them. Some are killed when they are only a few days old to be sold as low grade veal for frozen dinners and the like. The rest are slaughtered when they are 16 weeks old; they are frequently too sick or crippled to walk. Ten percent of veal cows die in confinement. They never see the sun, touch the Earth, or taste the grass.

Diseases Common to Veal Calves

- Chronic pneumonia

- Scours

- Anemia

Pigs

Sows

Female pigs are kept pregnant continually. After being impregnated, sows are placed in 18 to 24 inch wide pens or metal gestation crates. There is barely enough room for them to stand up and lie down. They cannot walk or turn around. Because straw is considered too expensive, they are not given bedding but instead forced to lie on hard floors which, in part, cause crippling leg disorders. Sometimes they are tied to the floor by a chain or strap. The pigs become so bored and stressed that they bite the bars of their cages frantically or rub their snouts back and forth across the front of their crate incessantly.

After giving birth, sows are only permitted to nurse their newborns for two to three weeks, as opposed to the 13 to 17 weeks they would naturally spend. The piglets are then taken away to be fattened up. By that time, approximately 15% of the newborns will have died. The sow is then reimpregnated, sometimes by being strapped to a "rape" table. When she can no longer breed at such a rapid pace, she is killed.

Piglets

Each piglet's tail is cut off without anesthesia so that other piglets will not bite it; tail biting is an unnatural behavior that results directly from the stress of the factory farm. For identification purposes, notches are removed from the piglets' ears. They are then placed in overcrowded pens with floors made of wire mesh, metal, fiberglass, or concrete. They are not given any straw or other bedding. The stress and disorder of such intense confinement drives some pigs to cannibalism. When they reach six months of age, they are slaughtered for their meat.

Diseases Common to Confined Pigs

- Pneumonia

- Porcine Reproductive and Respiratory Syndrome

- Miscellaneous respiratory diseases

- Swine arthritis

- Salmonellosis

- Epidemic transmissible gastroenteritis

- Bratislava

- Parvovirus

- Dysentery

- Cholera

- Trichinosis

The Slaughterhouse

Pigs are hung upside down by their back legs to be slaughtered. Because swine workers, like cattle workers, are in a rush to stay on schedule and kill a large number of animals in a short period of time, the pigs are often treated inhumanely. To accustom themselves to life at the slaughterhouse, workers must desensitize themselves to the animals' suffering and conceive of them as mere objects; this approach clearly leads to inhumane treatment. Moreover, the turnover rate at slaughterhouses is so high that there are a lot of new, inexperienced technicians who cannot properly sedate animals. Although pigs are supposed to be rendered unconscious before being killed, workers frequently do not successfully "stun" them. As a result, conscious, struggling pigs are hung upside down. If a worker does not successfully knife them in the neck, they are dunked in the scalding tank and boiled alive.

Horses

Every year, 100,000 horses are killed in U.S. slaughterhouses while others are shipped to Canada and Mexico to be killed. Former racehorses, carriage horses, draft horses, and abandoned pets are killed for their meat. In addition the manufacturers of Premarin, an estrogen replacement drug derived from pregnant mare urine, supply a number of horses for human consumption. The mares' offspring are raised for slaughter, and spent mares will also be killed for their meat.

Seafood

Farm-raised Fish

Fish, like all other vertebrates, feel pain. Farmed fish are crowded into such small enclosures that disease and suffocation are common. Since the water the fish swim in is filled with excrement and other health dangers, farmers feed fish chemicals, herbicides, and drugs, which end up in the bodies of fish-eating consumers. When the fish reach slaughter weight, they are placed in trucks and taken to the kill plant. Once there, they are poured into large metal mesh cages. Those who have survived the transport die of suffocation.

Downed animals ... are then usually dragged with chains and wenches or pushed with tractors or forklifts to the slaughterhouse or the "deadpile."

Wild Fishing

Wild fish species and populations have been destroyed by the seafood industry. Other sea life such as dolphins are often caught in fishermen's nets. This "by-catch," in the form of 80,000 marine mammals each year, is often dead when it is thrown back into the water.

Foie Gras

Foie gras is geese and duck liver which has been enlarged by forced-feeding. Workers generally force open ducks' bills and shove a long, metal pipe down their throats. Many of the ducks' stomachs burst from overfeeding. Infection, particularly pneumonia, is common since the same pipe is used on many ducks without being cleaned. They experience additional injuries as a result of being carried around by their necks.

Downed Animals

Downed animals are those that are so sick or injured that they cannot walk. They collapse in farms and stockyards and sometimes remain there for days. They are then usually dragged with chains and wenches or pushed with tractors or forklifts to the slaughterhouse or the "deadpile."

Free Range Farms

The United States Department of Agriculture, which regulates free-range products for labeling purposes, relies upon the producer's word that the farm animals are indeed free range. A farmer could therefore label a product "free-range" when in fact it is not. Moreover, there are very few requirements for labeling products "free range." For instance, birds raised for meat may be called "free-range" if they have some sort of access to the outdoors, regardless of how much space each individual animal has.

Free-range farm hens are unable to lay enough eggs to be considered profitable after one or two years. They are then typically sold to slaughterhouses or live-poultry markets (where Santeria practitioners often purchase animals to use in religious rituals). As on factory farms, free range, male chicks are considered worthless: At birth, they are dumped into trash cans and suffocated, ground up alive, or sold to laboratories.

And like factory farm animals, when free range animals can no longer produce, in other words, when they are no longer profitable, they are killed.

Leather

Some argue that there is no harm in wearing leather since the cows (or other animals) used to produce it are already dead, i.e. slaughtered for their meat. However, the animals are dead because there is a demand for their flesh and skin. If the demand for meat and leather decreases, fewer animals will be killed. Thus turning away from leather and toward more humane alternatives will save animal lives.

Leather is inextricably linked to the modern day factory farming system, an industrial process in which animals and the products they generate are mass-produced. The animals are seen not as individual, sentient beings with unique physical and psychological needs but as a means to an end—meat, leather, and so on. Because factory farming is a business, its goal is to maximize production and, consequently, profit. And since the animals are seen as mere commodities in this quest, they are bred, fed, confined, and drugged to lay more eggs, birth more offspring, and die with more meat on their bones. Farmers cut costs by feeding animals the remains of other animals, keeping them in extremely small and soiled enclosures, and refusing to provide bedding. Because animals live in such a manner and are denied normal social interactions, they experience boredom and stress so great that it leads to unnatural aggression and even self-mutilation. Most leather comes from factory farmed dairy cows and veal cows.

Some of the Animals Killed to Make Leather

- Cows

- Alligators

- Crocodiles

- Horses

- Sheep

- Lambs

- Pigs

- Goats

- Ostriches

- Dogs

- Cats

The Environment

Leather production harms the environment in several ways. First, tanning prevents leather from biodegrading. Tanneries use toxic substances to tan leather, and tannery effluent contains large amounts of other pollutants, such as protein, hair, salt, lime sludge, sulfides, and acids. Hazardous substances like formaldehyde, coal tar derivatives, mineral salts, oils, dyes and finishes are used to turn animal skin into leather; some of them are cyanide based. Tanneries release elevated levels of lead, cyanide, and formaldehyde into the ground water. Such high levels result in increased rates of leukemia.

The leather industry is inextricably tied to the meat industry, as the majority of cows used to make leather are dairy and veal cows who live on factory farms. Factory farms consume enormous quantities of fossil fuels, water, land, and other resources. They are filled with noxious fumes, dust, bacteria, and decaying feces, all of which they release into the environment. Animal wastes carry pesticides, bacteria and viruses; the wastes pollute drinking water with high levels of nitrates, which can be potentially fatal to infants.

Most People Are Unaware of How Much Suffering Factory Farming Causes Animals

Iris Sinilong

Iris Sinilong is a contributor to Urban Times, a news website that is based entirely on user-submitted content and that seeks to offer an alternative approach to issues from the mainstream media.

Currently, the process of eating meat is considered the norm in our culture. It is what is being portrayed by the media, through various advertisements, on a daily basis. We are consistently told that consuming meat is necessary for survival. Advertisements from companies like McDonald's, Kentucky Fried Chicken (KFC), Wendy's, and other food-chain restaurants reinforce this idea of meat consumption. However, things have not always been this way. It was not until the 1940s, after people discovered the benefits of injecting antibiotics and vitamin supplements on animals, that meat eating became more prevalent. In fact, in the past, meat consumption was reserved only for special occasions such as high days and holidays.

How Is Factory Farming Portrayed by the Media?

According to [French philosopher Michel] Foucault's theory on the power of discourse, the news media have an obligation to present the social issues surrounding the treatment of animals "fairly for public debate". In other words, it is the media's responsibility to present both the benefits and drawbacks of factory farms. It is the media's obligation to tell us what actually goes on inside every factory farm, and not hide behind the false pretenses that farm animals are happy and content. So is the news industry providing consumers with the truths about factory farms?

Most media for meat and dairy typically focus on the display of pastoral fields, green grass, and on animals roaming free. The media has instilled in our minds the idea that farm animals get the opportunity to graze, stride around, swish their tails, and moo or cluck in the open field, accompanied by a hard-working farmer with his family by his side. Every year, the meat industries spend billions of dollars on advertising and on devising strategies to influence the way we think about the food we eat. They offer free educational resources to schools, constantly broadcast advertisements on radio and TV stations, and they promote their products to doctors, nurses, and dieticians. In fact, in the past few years, there have been a growing number of partnerships between schools and fast-food chains. In 2008, McDonalds sponsored an elementary school in Seminole County by providing coupons alongside the children's report cards. Furthermore, they perpetuate the myth that animals are perfectly content by using packages that are decorated with pictures of happy animals. Egg cartons, for instance, are almost always seen carrying drawings of joyful hens, dancing under the blessing of a smiling sun.

Moreover, carnistic invisibility is employed through omission. This is the reason why the ten billions of animals that are killed each year for meat remain inconspicuous from public knowledge. The media intentionally hides the truth from us by leaving us little exposure to animals, and thus making it much easier to distance ourselves from the reality that our actions influence their treatment. Additionally, invisibility is maintained by actively preventing anticarnist information from reaching consumers. For example, in 2004, CBS turned down the $2-million deal with the animal rights group People for Ethical Treatment of Animals (PETA), which wanted to air an anti-meat advertisement during the Super Bowl. The network claimed that it did not support advocacy advertisements; yet, ironically, during the game, CBS ran an anti-smoking advertisement.

The Reality Behind Factory Farms

Currently, according to the statistics made by the United States Department of Agriculture (USDA), 10 billion animals are killed for food each year, which equals to:

- more than a million animals killed every hour
- 19,011 animals killed per minute
- 317 animals killed per second

What Happens Inside Factory Farms?

For the most part, animals in factory farms are in confinement buildings, which have a glass viewing port where the visitor, as well as the farmer, can view the animals. The reality also is that most animals are penned up all day and night, with the amount of sunshine scientifically controlled. There is also automation to provide the animals with food, water, and an occasional change of air, so the farmer may not even need to "visit" his animals more than once a day. In addition, the media does not disclose the amount of suffering that actually goes on in every factory farm. They do not tell us that chickens are the most tortured animals in factory farms and that most chickens have to stand on their own feces all day and end up getting litter burn from their manure. The fact that layer hens are often crammed together in cases so tiny that they do not get enough room to even lift a single wing—which then immobilizes them for their entire lives—are also hidden from us. Moreover, when egg production declines, the hens are often subjected to a process called "forced molting";

in which they are starved and denied water to shock the hens into losing their feathers so those that survive can start a new laying cycle.

Factory farms' employees ... develop serious respiratory diseases, reproductive dysfunction, neurological degeneration, seizures, and comas.

Although many people are now aware of what veal calves are, many are still oblivious to the amount of suffering they go through for society to have an enjoyable dinner. In fact, many are unaware that veal calves are kept in total darkness for most of any given day, fed a diet of iron-deficient milk substitute, and are often left to starve, so as to produce a product whose flesh is palatably pale and tender. Most pigs (more than millions of them), on the other hand, spend their entire lives in intensive confinement and never see outdoors until they are packed into trucks to be sent to slaughter. This is unfortunate considering just how intelligent and friendly pigs actually are. As a matter of fact, it only takes piglets 3 weeks to remember names and to respond when called. However, not a lot of people know about this because the media has been so focused on objectifying them.

Other Disadvantages

What is often undocumented is the fact that animals are not only the ones affected by factory farms.

- Factory farms' employees, who are routinely exposed to noxious gases from concentrated wastes, usually develop serious respiratory diseases, reproductive dysfunction, neurological degeneration, seizures, and comas.

- Residents who live near factory farms are affected through the toxins that contaminate the air and their drinking water which lead to eye irritation, chronic asthma, bronchitis, diarrhea, severe headaches, nausea, spontaneous abortions, birth defects, infant death, and viral and bacterial disease outbreaks.

- Approximately two-thirds of the 1,400 known human pathogens originated in animals.

- Scientific studies and government records also suggest that almost all chickens are infected with E. coli and about 39 to 75 percent of these chickens that are transported to retail stores are still infected.

Furthermore, the livestock industry accounts for:

- 80% of the greenhouse gas emission, while the

- methane produced by cattle and their manure has a global warming effect equivalent to that of 33 million automobiles.

So Why Do People [Not] Reject the Disastrous Effects of Factory Farming?

When it comes to food choices, most of us turn to what our habits dictate. "There is ease and relaxation in doing what we have always done. And if our habits are continually reinforced by the society around us, they can become even more powerful and alluring." In addition, it is simply much easier to eat meat than to avoid it. Meat is always readily available. Non-meat alternatives, on the other hand, are much harder to find. You have to actively seek them. On top of it all, vegetarians are often faced with the dilemma of having "to explain their choices, defend their diet, and apologize for inconveniencing others". Many individuals are aware that the meat we consumes come from animals. However, society does not want to concede the horrors because they do not want to acknowledge the connection between their actions and the animal's sufferings. Others detach themselves from the harsh realities of factory farming by avoiding questions that lead to the optimal truths about factory farms. Since embracing these disguises can "shield us not only from the fact that it is dead (mostly baby) animals that we are eating, but they also obscure the moral and epistemic obligation to know how our actions may contribute, in some way, to another's suffering". . . .

It is important to consider the ethical issues relating [to] factory farming since [the] majority of our food comes from industrial farms. Also, once we are able to make full empathetic connections to the food we eat, we would then be able to make wiser decisions. Meat eating was not as prevalent 60 or 70 years ago, so why should it be now?

The Pork Industry Hides Its Abuse of Pigs

Joseph Mercola

Joseph Mercola is an alternative physician from Illinois, the author of several books, and a contributor of health-related articles to many online and other media resources.

A ridiculous video from the Pork Producers Council attempts to explain why factory pig farming is a wonderful thing.

They say they put up "modern" barns to protect animals from harsh weather, illness and predators . . . which when translated to reality means the pigs never get to see the light of day, are packed in so tightly, living in their own feces, that illness runs rampant, and as for predators, well, the farm workers themselves are often caught in acts of abuse.

The idyllic cartoon farm pictured in the video above [available on Mercola.com] is a far cry from the typical confined animal feeding operation (CAFO), which can house tens of thousands of animals (and in the case of chickens, 100,000) under one roof, in nightmarish, unsanitary, disease-ridden conditions.

What Does a Typical Swine CAFO Look Like?

You may be surprised to learn that pigs are more intelligent than dogs.

Their cognitive ability is even greater than most 3-year-old children.

If given the chance, pigs are social and playful, and they spend their days rooting for insects, grazing on grass, and rolling in the mud.

The vast majority of the nearly 66 million pigs raised for food in the United States never experience this life, however, as they are born and raised in CAFOs, where they are subject to mental and physical anguish, not to mention subject to incredibly unhealthy practices, like the administration of unnecessary low-dose antibiotics and living in their own waste, which impacts whoever ends up eating the meat as well as the environment. . . .

Unfortunately, even though most food comes from facilities that resemble factories rather than farms, many Americans still believe their food is grown on small family farm like the ones in the above video. This is exactly what the Ohio Pork Producers Council, and other industrial agribusiness giants, want you to believe.

Because if you *really* knew where your pork, chicken or beef had come from, there's a very strong chance you would not only refuse to eat it, but would be incredibly appalled at the very thought. . . .

There's Nothing "Neighborly" About a CAFO . . .

The Pork Producers Council had the audacity to massively misstate that their farms are designed to protect the environment and be good neighbors. Swine CAFOs are notorious for the odors they produce. Living in the nearby vicinity to one is akin to living next to a landfill or a chemical factory, maybe even worse. It's not unusual for people to report the fumes coming from the CAFOs are so bad they can't make it from their house to their car without stopping to retch. This isn't only a matter of bad odor, though; it's a serious health threat. . . .

There are other serious problems as well, including drinking water contamination from the massive amounts of animal waste generated on CAFOs. . . .

Pork Consumption Is Linked to Liver Damage, Other Health Problems

I am not opposed to eating meat, as long as it comes from a healthy source and is cooked properly (which is lightly or not at all), but there is reason to carefully consider whether pork should be a part of your diet, regardless of the source.

An infectious pathogen in pork is responsible for the associated health conditions including liver disease and multiple sclerosis.

Pork consumption has a strong epidemiological association with cirrhosis of the liver—in fact, it may be more strongly associated with cirrhosis than alcohol (although some have questioned the studies that indicate this, and point out that countries with high pork consumption tend to have low obesity rates). Other studies also show an association between pork consumption and liver cancer as well as multiple sclerosis. However, this may be more related to the way that the pork is raised than the actually toxicity of the meat.

Most pigs raised in the United States are fed grains and possibly seed oils, which dramatically increase their omega-6 content, as well as the highly inflammatory byproduct of omega-6 fatty acid metabolism: arachadonic acid. According to the Weston A. Price Foundation, lard from pigs fed this type of diet may be 32 percent PUFAs [poly unsaturated fats acids]. On the other hand, lard from pigs raised on pasture and acorns had a much lower PUFA content, at 8.7 percent, while those fed a Pacific Island diet rich in coconut had even less, only 3.1 percent. . . .

Consumption of this PUFA-rich meat may very well be a factor in liver disease, as studies show feeding mice corn oil (rich in omega-6) and alcohol (which is metabolically similar to fructose) induces liver disease and omega-6 fats have also been linked to cirrhosis of the liver. Ironically, despite this known connection, Dr. [Paul] Jaminet reports that liver cancer appears to be even more strongly associated with the consumption of *fresh* pork than processed pork, which suggests another causative factor. Dr. Jaminet suggests that an infectious pathogen in pork is responsible for the associated health conditions including liver disease and multiple sclerosis. . .

So this is an area that you will have to make up your own mind about. All I can do is present you with the evidence and you can make your own decision. There are many bright people in natural medicine who believe organic healthy raised pork is a health food and other experts agree even that is best avoided. Personally, I like to err on the side of caution and do severely limit my pork intake, but I will have it occasionally. I never eat ham lunchmeat and avoid pork chops and ham roasts but do enjoy nitrate-free sausage occasionally.

Corporate-owned CAFOs have been highly promoted as the best way to produce food for the masses.

U.S. Government Supports CAFOs Over Small Family Farms

The U.S. government has a history of supporting CAFOs, both by looking the other way when abuse or contamination occurs, and by directly subsidizing cheaply produced beef, and corn and soy used for feed. For instance, in December 2011 police raided a North Carolina Butterball turkey farm after hidden camera video obtained by the animal rights group

Mercy for Animals showed workers kicking and stomping on turkeys, as well as injured birds with open wounds and exposed flesh.

But the company knew in advance the raid was coming, as phone records show a veterinarian at the *North Carolina Department of Agriculture* tipped off a veterinarian employed by Butterball about the coming raid. . . .

Corporate-owned CAFOs have been highly promoted as the best way to produce food for the masses, but the only reason CAFOs are able to remain so "efficient," bringing in massive profits while selling their food for bottom-barrel prices, is because they substitute subsidized crops for pasture grazing.

Factory farms use massive quantities of corn, soy and grain in their animal feed, all crops that they are often able to purchase at below cost because of government subsidies. Because of these subsidies, U.S. farmers produce massive amounts of soy, corn, wheat, etc.—rather than vegetables— leading to a monoculture of foods that contribute to a fast food diet. . . .

As it stands, the book [*CAFO: The Tragedy of Industrial Animal Factories*] notes that "grazing and growing feed for livestock now occupy 70 percent of all agricultural land and 30 percent of the ice-free terrestrial surface of the planet. If present trends continue, meat production is predicted to double between the turn of the 21st century and 2050." Does this sound sustainable to you?

There Are Better Places to Get Your Meat

I encourage you to support the small family farms in your area, particularly *organic* farms that respect the laws of nature and use the relationships between animals, plants, insects, soil, water and habitat to create synergistic, self-supporting, non-polluting, GMO [genetically modified organism]-free ecosystems.

Whether you do so for ethical, environmental or health reasons—or all of the above—the closer you can get to the "backyard barnyard," the better. You'll want to get your meat, chickens and eggs from smaller community farms with free-ranging animals, organically fed and locally marketed. This is the way food has been raised and distributed for centuries . . . before it was corrupted by politics, corporate greed and the blaring arrogance of the food industry.

You can do this not only by visiting the farm directly, if you have one nearby, but also by taking part in farmer's markets and community-supported agriculture programs.

CHAPTER 3

Does Factory Farming Harm Human Health or the Environment?

Chapter Preface

Many observers and environmental experts agree that large farm animal operations defined by US law as concentrated animal feeding operations (CAFOs) comprise a potent source of water and air pollution in the United States. Raising thousands of animals inside buildings produces tons of animal wastes and other pollutants that typically are discharged into the soil, water, and air surrounding these facilities. Yet federal regulation of CAFOs is still relatively weak according to many commentators.

First passed in 1972, the Clean Water Act (CWA) is one of the strongest sources of regulation for CAFOs. Broadly speaking, this law prohibits the discharge of pollution into US waters from any source unless authorized by a permit issued by the Environmental Protection Agency (EPA). CAFOs are defined as a source of pollution under the CWA, but attempts by the EPA to address CAFO water pollution have often been challenged in court by livestock and poultry trade organizations seeking to weaken government regulation efforts. The result, according to environmentalists, is that EPA regulations of CAFOs under the CWA remain ineffectual.

Two examples, one from 2008 and the other from 2012, illustrate how the EPA has failed to restrict CAFOs. In 2008 the EPA issued regulations that required CAFOs that propose to discharge pollutants into US waters to first obtain a Clean Water Act National Pollutant Discharge Elimination System (NPDES) permit that imposes limitations on the amount of discharge and imposes other requirements for controlling water pollution. EPA rules stipulated that CAFOs propose to discharge pollutants whenever they are constructed, operated, or maintained in a way that makes a discharge likely. This stipulation covers most, if not all, CAFOs; however, CAFOs could seek exemption from the permit requirement by arguing that they would not discharge pollutants. If CAFOs discharged without applying for the NPDES permit, the EPA provided for penalties to be assessed. Animal producers' trade associations (including the National Pork Producers Council, the National Chicken Council, the US Poultry & Egg Association, the Dairy Business Association, Inc., and others) challenged these EPA regulations in a lawsuit, *National Pork Producers Council v. EPA*, filed in federal court. The US Court of Appeals for the Fifth Circuit ruled in favor of the plaintiffs, finding that CWA does not require CAFOs to apply for a NPDES permit before a discharge occurs because the EPA lacks authority over CAFOs until there is an actual discharge of pollutants. The EPA was thus forced to modify its regulations to eliminate the requirement that CAFOS that propose to discharge must apply for a permit, a change that was issued in a final EPA rule effective July 30, 2012.

Although some CAFOs may choose to apply for a permit before discharging pollutants under current regulations, environmental advocates suspect that CAFOs are more likely to dump their wastes without a permit in the hopes that they will not be caught or wait until the last minute before applying for a permit, in hopes that the discharge will occur before EPA acts on the permit request. Advocates also charge that the 2008 regulation was already limited because it did not cover animal wastes applied on land not under the CAFO operator's control or land dumping of pollutants such as heavy metals, antibiotics, pathogens, growth hormones, or other substances typically found in CAFO wastes.

In July 2012, another victory for CAFOs occurred. The EPA announced that it was withdrawing a proposed CWA regulation that would have required CAFOs to report information to the government, such as type of facility, number and type of animals housed in the facility, whether the CAFO dumps waste on land, available acreage available for land waste application, and whether the CAFO has a NPDES permit. This regulation had been considered necessary because the US Government Accountability Office (GAO) noted in a 2008 report that no federal agency collects consistent, accurate information about CAFOs, information needed to make sure wastes are handled in a way that minimizes water pollution.

CAFOs could potentially be regulated under other federal laws too. The Clean Air Act (CAA), for example, regulates air pollution, and CAFOs are known to release toxic gases such as ammonia into the air. In June 2012, under pressure from environmental groups, the EPA took the first step toward regulating CAFO air pollution by proposing draft measurement tools, called Emissions Estimating Methodologies, designed to estimate the quantities of toxic pollutants released by large animal operations. The methodologies are based on a study proposed in 2002, which investigated twenty-one CAFO facilities such as chicken broiler producers and large dairy and hog operations. In order to get industry cooperation, the EPA granted amnesty from enforcement of clean air laws to fourteen thousand CAFO facilities that contributed to study costs and agreed to participate if chosen for the study. Environmental groups praised the EPA effort as a positive step forward, but as of early 2013, CAFOs remain unregulated under the CAA.

Another federal agency with jurisdiction over CAFOs is the US Food and Drug Administration (FDA). CAFOs have been criticized for overusing antibiotics, which help prevent disease and encourage growth in farm animals. Critics charge that this widespread factory farm practice causes some types of bacteria to become resistant to antibiotics, rendering them useless when prescribed to treat humans. In response to a federal court ruling in a lawsuit filed by an environmental group, *Natural Resources Defense Council, Inc. v. US Food & Drug Administration*, the FDA on April 11, 2012, proposed rules relating to antibiotics fed to animals. The FDA rule requires a prescription from a veterinarian in an effort to make sure that antibiotics will only be used for disease treatment and prevention and not to enhance animal growth. In addition, the FDA recommends that factory farms phase out the use of certain types of antibiotics important in treating humans and asks drug companies to voluntarily label antibiotic drugs to eliminate the use of such drugs by factory farms for animal growth enhancement or other so-called production purposes. Critics argued that voluntary rules do not work, but government representatives vowed to impose stricter rules in the future if voluntary means are ineffective.

The authors of viewpoints in this chapter discuss the various ways in which CAFOs and animal factory farms affect human health and the environment.

Factory Farms Are Contaminating US Drinking Water

Karen Steuer

Karen Steuer is the director of government relations for the Pew Charitable Trusts. The group works to protect the oceans, save wildlands, and promote a clean energy economy.

During the last 50 years, animal agriculture has gone through a seismic shift in the U.S. Long gone are the iconic scenes of American landscapes dotted with family farms and red barns. Most of these have been replaced by industrialized facilities controlled by large corporations that rely on concentrated animal feeding operations (CAFOs). In this system, cavernous warehouses crowded with thousands—even tens of thousands—of animals form the equivalent of an agricultural assembly line. And independent farmers, once the cornerstone of rural America, struggle to compete in a marketplace dominated by a few big corporations.

CAFO Problems

As large corporations (known as integrators) have applied an industrial model to farming, they have also generated a host of new problems.

The CAFO model relies on three interlinked practices in order to increase profits:

- Maximize the number of animals squeezed into the least amount of space and require the fewest number of employees to provide care.

- Administer continual doses of antibiotics to the animals to prevent the diseases prevalent in their close-quarters housing.

- Minimize the disposal cost for the substantial volume of animal waste produced by the facilities.

These practices may turn a profit for the big corporations, but they are disastrous for human health and the environment. Up to 1 billion tons of manure is generated by livestock operations every year, much of it from CAFOs. In some cases, the waste is stored in large lagoons or open piles that can leak or spill into adjacent land and water. In other cases, manure is liberally spread on fields in such overwhelming concentrations that soil and crops often cannot impede all of the nitrogen, phosphorus and pathogens from reaching public waterways.

The mishandling of manure has resulted in contaminated drinking water sources for 40 percent of the U.S. population in recent years, according to Environmental Protection Agency [EPA] estimates. Tainted drinking water, destruction of fish and other aquatic life, and polluted recreation areas, however, are just part of the damage caused by CAFOs.

Countless independent farmers have been pushed out of business. Millions of animals have been confined to crates or cages and subjected to inhumane practices. The human health threat of antibiotic-resistant infections continues to rise. And the corporate integrators have largely been insulated from regulation, transparency, and requirements many other industries must follow with regard to pollution.

Shortly after the Pew Commission on Industrial Farm Animal Production released a groundbreaking report on this topic in 2008, the Pew Charitable Trusts launched a campaign aimed at reforming this sector of agriculture. Pew is working to address these challenges by securing effective, sensible government oversight to protect water resources and human health, urging the industry to change its practices and building public awareness of the problems.

During the next several months [following June 2012], I will use this series to describe the environmental concerns associated with CAFOs, the impact on independent farmers, the industry's resistance to change and how this issue affects our quality of life in the U.S.

The US Environmental Protection Agency Is Moving Toward Better Regulation of Factory Farm Air Pollution

Center for Food Safety

The Center for Food Safety is a nonprofit environmental advocacy organization that seeks to end harmful food production technologies and promote sustainable alternatives.

The Center for Food Safety, Environmental Integrity Project, Center on Race, Poverty & the Environment, Sierra Club and others submitted recommendations to the Environmental Protection Agency (EPA) today [June 12, 2012], commending its first step towards measuring and regulating air pollution from factory farms, and suggesting improvements to make those measurements more accurate and more protective of public health and quality of life in rural areas.

Measuring Factory Farm Air Pollution

The draft measurement tools, referred to as "Emissions Estimating Methodologies" [EEMs], are EPA's first attempt to estimate the quantities of toxic gases—including ammonia, hydrogen sulfide, particulates, and volatile organic compounds—emitted by large livestock operations. EPA based the methodologies on an industry-sponsored study of 21 operations. The factory farm industry proposed the study in 2002, and EPA agreed to grant amnesty from enforcement of clean air laws to nearly 14,000 facilities in exchange for each facility's contribution to study costs and agreement to participate in the study if selected. This first set of draft methodologies covers emissions from broiler houses and open waste pits at megadairy and hog operations.

Environmental Integrity Project Attorney Tarah Heinzen said: "Establishing estimates for factory farm air pollution is a step in the right direction to regulating air emissions to protect public health and the environment. In order to make this a truly effective reform, however, EPA must clarify that all factory farms—not only those that signed up for EPA's sweetheart deal in 2005—will be required to report emissions estimates and comply with clean air laws without further delay."

The draft methodologies for the broiler chicken sector indicate that a typical facility with at least 4 chicken houses will exceed the 100 pound per day reporting threshold for ammonia, a requirement that would likely apply to hundreds of facilities in the Chesapeake Bay watershed. In addition to providing data and reducing health impacts, the estimates will help EPA measure and reduce ammonia emissions that redeposit into waterways—a major source of nitrogen pollution in the Chesapeake Bay and other critical water resources.

Despite the small scale of EPA's emissions study, the agency has refused to consider other peer-reviewed data. "EPA agreed to consider all relevant information in drafting the EEMs, and it has not," said Elisabeth Holmes, attorney for the Center for Food Safety. "By neglecting existing, reliable science, the government appears to be willfully ducking documentation that would improve the accuracy and usefulness of its emissions estimates, benefiting public health and the environment. EPA can do better."

The groups also expressed concern over the complexity of the proposed methods, noting that factory farm operators will have to use the tools and report their own emissions. EPA's Science Advisory Board established an expert committee to review the highly technical draft methodologies, but the report had not been finalized before the end of public comment. The environmental groups urged EPA to re-open the comment period once this information becomes available.

Factory Farms Are Weakening the Effectiveness of Antibiotics

Lynne Peeples

Lynne Peeples is a journalist who writes about the environment and public health for The Huffington Post, *an online news and commentary publication.*

Waste from people, pets, pigs and even seagulls may be playing a significant role in the rise of antibiotic-resistant infections, including methicillin-resistant Staphylococcus aureus (MRSA), a number of new studies warn.

Widespread fear of diminishing returns for modern medicine is becoming amplified, scientists say, by the discovery of soils and waterways polluted with both traces of antibiotics and bacteria encoded with antibiotic-resistant genes, the information that tells a microbe how to evade drugs designed to kill it. And even if that fortified microbe isn't capable of causing illness in humans itself, scientists add, its DNA could find its way into the more malignant microbes in the environment.

"Antibiotic resistance is likely the biggest public health challenge that we'll be facing this century," said Amy Pruden, an expert on antibiotic resistance at Virginia Tech. "We're in a state of complacency right now. We count on antibiotics working for us, but they are slowly starting to lose their effectiveness."

Antibiotics in the Environment

While progress has been made in the clinical realm—limiting unnecessary uses of antibiotics, for example, and encouraging patients to take the full course of their prescribed drugs—

Pruden noted "mounting evidence that the environment is another important piece of the puzzle."

Drug residues and bacteria with drug-resistant genes can pass together through a human's or animal's gut and into the environment, even if the living contaminants take a detour through a wastewater treatment plant.

Bacteria can easily swap genes with each other.

In a study published on Tuesday [May 9, 2012], Scottish researchers found that relatively low concentrations of antibiotics in certain environments—such as river sediments, swine feces lagoons and farmed soil—may be enough to speed along the proliferation of the drug-resistant genes. It's another survival-of-the-fittest story: Bacteria that can withstand the drugs will survive and reproduce, while their antibiotic-susceptible counterparts die out.

The winning genes then have the potential to infiltrate drinking water or produce, which increases human exposure and raises the likelihood that the genes will spread.

"Antibiotic resistance is such a big global health concern," said Alfredo Tello of the University of Stirling, lead researcher on the study. "We need to consider the effect that antibiotics released into the environment can have on development of this resistance."

Adding to the danger is the fact that bacteria can easily swap genes with each other. A bacterium that passes through the intestines into the local waterway, for example, may not itself be a pathogen that normally threatens human health, but that benign bug can share its drug-tolerating secrets.

"It's not necessarily important what species is holding on to the DNA as long as the DNA is held on to and propagated," explained David Cummings, a biologist at Point Loma Nazarene University in San Diego. "Then it can later be released to cause disease in an animal, plant or human."

Cummings' own research has identified dangerous DNA in the river sediments around San Diego and across the Mexican border into Tijuana.

"These coastal wetland habitats are becoming sinks and ultimately sources for drug-resistant bacteria—more importantly, sinks for the DNA that provide resistance," said Cummings, who points his finger at pet waste, bird feces, leaky sewer pipes and hospital waste effluent as the likely culprits in the San Diego area, which is home to few livestock operations. "We've tinkered with a lot of resistance genes, and anything we look for, we find."

A separate study published last month [April 2012] also emphasized the importance of oft-overlooked aquatic sources of antibiotic resistance. Canadian researchers analyzed four different bodies of water affected by varying levels of human activity. They found resistance genes at all four sites, although the intensity varied: A harbor hosting sewer overflows suffered from higher levels than a nature preserve.

"Antibiotic resistance is widespread in aquatic environments ranging from heavily impacted urban sites to remote areas," Lesley Warren of McMaster University in Canada, and the lead researcher on the study, said in a statement. "The presence of environmental bacterial communities in aquatic environments represents a significant, largely unknown source of antibiotic resistance."

What's more, antibiotic residue and resistance genes may be spread farther and more widely by wildlife, particularly seabirds. Researchers at the University of Miami [Florida] recently found a large number of seagulls and pelicans were host to bacteria associated with broad-spectrum resistance to infectious bugs, such as the *E. coli* that causes urinary tract infections in women.

It is becoming increasingly evident that the world's dire antibiotic-resistance problem involves a lot of players, all acting through a variety of complicated means. So what should be done?

"The solutions need to come from upstream, figuratively and literally," said Cummings. "That can be public education, improving our wastewater management and treatment—even something as simple, albeit expensive, as separating stormwater from the sewage system." The latter would limit the untreated sewage flowing into waterways.

The Antibiotic Problem with Livestock

Of course, excrement from livestock is subject to even looser waste management practices than human waste. The use of antibiotics in livestock is the subject of ongoing debate. According to the latest estimates from the U.S. Food and Drug Administration [FDA], 80 percent of the country's antibiotics are given to food animals, predominantly for the purpose of promoting growth or preventing disease, rather than for treating illness.

Also published this Tuesday was a study implicating the widespread use of antibiotics in swine feed. Not only do antibiotic-resistant genes end up in the soil and wastewater around the feedlots, but researchers suggest the genes are often spread further by the application of the waste on crop lands.

In response to the growing concerns, the FDA released contentious guidelines last month that ask pork, beef and poultry producers to choose to stop using antibiotics for fattening up their livestock. As *The Huffington Post* reported in March [2012], the agency has also been ordered by a federal court to follow through on a rule proposed in 1977 that would withdraw approvals for most non-therapeutic uses of penicillin and tetracyclines in livestock, drugs particularly crucial in human medicine.

"Every time you use antibiotics, you can select for resistance," said Gail Hansen, senior officer with the Pew Campaign on Human Health and Industrial Farming. "When giving them to healthy animals for no reason other than to get them to grow faster or compensate for unhygienic conditions, you're adding to that."

"The new research," added Hansen, "really points out that antibiotics aren't just affecting the bacteria while they're inside the pig."

What Is the Future of Factory Farming?

Chapter Preface

Among the criticisms faced by factory farm owners is their use of lean finely textured beef (LFTB) in US-produced ground beef, a practice that came under fire in the media in March 2012 when *ABC News* broadcast a report that referred to LFTB as pink slime. The *ABC* report also described LFTB as a substance once used only in dog food and cooking oils that is now used in human food after it is sprayed with ammonia to make it safe to eat. Many consumers reacted to this and other media reports by questioning the quality and safety of LFTB ground beef additives. Previous publicity about LFTB led to decisions by three large fast-food restaurants (McDonald's, Burger King, and Taco Bell) to stop using LFTB meat. This latest LFTB controversy placed more pressure on meat producers. In September 2012, the largest manufacturer of LFTB fought back by filing a defamation lawsuit against *ABC News*, former US Department of Agriculture (USDA) workers, and others who criticized the LFTB product.

LFTB is a beef product developed by Beef Products Inc. (BPI) in 1991 to make ground beef more lean. It is used in other meat products, including lunch meats, sausage, and hot dogs. LFTB is produced from beef trimmings, from which the fat is extracted, and the resulting beef is treated with ammonium gas to kill pathogens such as *E. coli*. The US Food and Drug Administration (FDA) approved the use of ammonium hydroxide gas as safe in 1983, and after that it was used either directly in or in the processing of various food products, such as baked goods, dairy products, and breakfast cereals. Similarly, the US Department of Agriculture approved both the use of LFTB in ground beef and the ammonium process used to treat LFTB, and LFTB has been used in meat purchased for the National School Lunch Program. Industry experts have estimated that up to 70 percent of all ground beef sold in the United States contains LFTB.

The negative characterization of LFTB as pink slime actually began more than ten years before the 2012 report in comments made by two USDA employees who opposed the agency's approval of the ammonium hydroxide process. One of the employees called LFTB pink slime and also stated that it was fraudulent to label ground beef that had been blended with LFTB as ground beef. These comments were uncovered when the *New York Times* filed a Freedom of Information Act (FOIA) request during its investigation and reporting on LFTB in 2009. The pink slime characterization was later repeated by various media sources, including *ABC News*.

Although questions had been raised earlier about LFTB, the negative publicity surrounding LFTB in 2012 caused consumers once again to question whether LFTB and the ammonium gas process are safe and whether the use of LFTB in ground beef should be labeled. The strongest criticism came from parents who worried about LFTB being fed to their children in schools. The first result of this public outcry was a decision on March 15, 2012, by the USDA to give school districts the option to stop buying LFTB-infused ground beef, although the agency at the same time affirmed that LFTB is a safe product. Members of Congress responded by urging the USDA to require labeling of LFTB ground beef. In addition, some large grocery chain stores such as Safeway announced that they would no longer buy LFTB ground beef products; others such as COSTCO and Whole Foods noted that they already did not carry LFTB beef; and still others such as Walmart planned to offer its customers a choice between LFTB and non-LFTB ground beef. Some meat producers have also voluntarily begun to put labels on their meat products indicating whether they contain LFTB. These actions have caused a sharp drop in prices for beef trimmings, the main ingredient used to make LFTB, and many commentators predict that a reduction in the use of LFTB could produce much higher ground beef prices. Such an outcome could place yet another cost burden on consumers, who depend on ground beef as a low-cost meat and protein source for their families.

Perhaps the biggest impact of the LFTB controversy fell on BPI, the nation's main manufacturer of the product. Because of the decline in demand, BPI shut down three of its four LFTB processing plants and laid off six hundred-fifty employees. On September 13, 2012, BPI announced that it was filing a lawsuit against *ABC News*, former USDA officials, and a former BPI employee for alleged defamation of its LFTB product. The lawsuit seeks $1.2 billion in damages and claims that *ABC* and other defendants carried out a campaign against BPI that caused consumers to conclude that LFTB is unsafe and fraudulently labeled.

Many commentators say that the LFTB controversy is an example of how modern food production techniques can be misunderstood by consumers. BPI and meat producers argue that LFTB is a completely safe product and a cost-efficient way to decrease the fat in ground beef. This technology, supporters say, provides consumers with a healthier ground beef option at a lower price. Critics of LFTB, however, worry about the use of processed meat in ground beef and argue that it lowers the standards for what should be an unadulterated, fresh beef product. The authors of the viewpoints included in this chapter discuss other pressures or changes that may lie ahead for factory farms in the future.

Agriculture Must Adopt More Sustainable Farming Methods

Union of Concerned Scientists

The Union of Concerned Scientists is a science-based nonprofit organization that advocates for a healthy environment and a safer world.

Ever wonder why it costs less to fill up your grocery cart with corn chips and sugary drinks than carrots and squash? In large part, it's because government policies make the wrong foods cheaper and more abundant by providing billions of dollars in subsidies for processed food ingredients like corn syrup. These ill-conceived subsidies give processed foods an unfair advantage over fruits, vegetables, pasture-raised meats, and other healthy foods.

And the same thing is happening with farming practices: federal policies subsidize agricultural operations that use millions of tons of toxic chemicals, damaging the soil, water, and air—along with our health in the process. Precious taxpayer dollars also fund research that maintains and expands this industrial system.

Instead of subsidizing processed food and pollution, we need to support healthy food and farms, and that will require forward-thinking farm and food policies. Every five years or so, Congress renews what is commonly referred to as the Farm Bill, a package of federal legislation that includes subsidies for various crops and farming practices, low-income food programs, incentives for farmers to protect and conserve their soil and water, investments in agricultural research, and more.

The Farm Bill offers a unique opportunity to change what the nation's farmers grow—and how they grow it—for years to come.

Our industrialized, highly processed food system . . . drains the nation's energy resources.

The Problem of Industrial Agriculture

In today's food system, short-term productivity and big corporate profits win out over our health and environment. Decades of shortsighted farm bills have led to an agriculture designed to produce massive quantities of a few crops. In 2010, the U.S. Department of Agriculture (USDA) paid out more than $5 billion in subsidies for just two processed-food and animal-feed crops: corn and soybeans.

And while the USDA urges Americans to eat more fruits and vegetables, farmers receive few incentives to grow them. Subsidies for all fruits and vegetables amount to only about 7 percent of what corn and soy receive. Nutritious, environmentally friendly pasture-raised meats—which, unlike meats produced in highly polluting CAFOs (confined animal feeding operations), do not rely on subsidized feed crops—get almost no support.

Large-scale, chemical-intensive methods of food production damage the natural resources on which we depend. According to the U.S. Environmental Protection Agency [EPA], agriculture is the leading source of water pollution in the nation's rivers and streams, and a major contributor to the contamination of lakes, reservoirs, and groundwater supplies. The industry's practices poison fish and shellfish; expose farm workers, consumers, and wildlife to toxic pesticides; degrade the soil for future generations of farmers. Our industrialized, highly processed food system also drains the nation's energy resources, accounting for nearly 16 percent of all the energy used in the United States.

Today's farm and food policy incentives are skewed toward this harmful industrial model, but they don't have to be. We can—and must—transition to a system that helps farmers profit by producing affordable, nutritious foods while minimizing energy use and pollution.

The Science of Sustainable Agriculture

The Union of Concerned Scientists (UCS) has a science-based vision for the U.S. farming and food system in which farms are not factories, and do not rely heavily on fossil fuels, harmful pesticides, and synthetic fertilizers to produce huge quantities of just a few crops. Instead, farmers and policy makers aim to produce a wide variety of nutritious foods while taking the long-term environmental and health impacts of production methods into account.

This vision of a truly sustainable agriculture employs the science of *agroecology*, which utilizes knowledge from the biological sciences and views farms as ecosystems that comprise interacting elements including soil, plants, insects, water, and animals. Each element in this system can be modified to solve problems, maximize yields, and conserve resources.

Farms managed using agroecological principles may use a variety of sophisticated practices including:

- Longer crop rotations and a wider variety of crops, which help maintain soil fertility and keep pest populations down so farmers need fewer pesticides;

- Raising crops and livestock in close proximity, which supplies feed (forage crops as well as grains) for the animals and nutrients (in the form of manure) for the soil, maintaining productivity while reducing waste, pollution, and transportation costs;-

- Cover cropping, in which an off-season crop helps protect soil from erosion and reduces the need for added fertilizer, minimizing pollution.

We can take significant steps forward by adopting and expanding innovative policies grounded in the latest science and economics.

Organic agriculture in particular borrows heavily from the agroecological approach. In place of chemical pesticides and fertilizers, certified organic farmers must rely on healthier soil and more diverse ecosystems to produce safe, abundant food. These methods have been refined through scientific investigation of the interactions within ecosystems, and sometimes use cutting-edge technologies to achieve results.

Agricultural researchers have indicated that organic and agroecological systems can meet the world's food needs while protecting and enhancing the environment. But according to a three-year global assessment involving hundreds of experts, this will entail a radical transformation of existing food and farming systems. A 2010 United Nations report urges all countries to quickly expand the scale of sustainable farming systems.

Policies for Real Food and Healthy Farms

The U.S. food and farm landscape will not be transformed overnight. But we *can* take significant steps forward by adopting and expanding innovative policies grounded in the latest science and economics.

In particular, UCS supports farm policies that will:

Expand the production and accessibility of healthy food. Appropriate tools include:

- Increased investment in local and regional food systems—including farmers markets, community-supported agriculture (CSA) arrangements, and food hubs—that will increase access for consumers across all income levels;

- New incentives for farmers to produce more organic, sustainable, and healthy food, especially fruits and vegetables; and

- A "safety net" of credit and risk management tools to support farmers who adopt sustainable and diversified practices.

Increase farmers' adoption of sustainable agriculture and conservation practices that protect soil, water, human health, and ecosystems. This can be done through:

- Greater financial incentives for farmers who implement conservation measures and adopt science-based sustainable, organic, and integrated crop or livestock production practices and systems;

- New rules that ensure farmers receiving federal subsidies employ at least a minimum level of conservation and limit their use of environmentally destructive practices.

Increase publicly funded research to improve and expand modern, sustainable food and farm systems. This research should seek to:

- Increase understanding of the ecosystems that support farming and the impacts of various management systems, practices, and technologies;

- Develop and refine innovative systems for sustainable, organic, and diversified food production, and ease farmers' transitions to them;

- Foster the expansion of local and regional food systems, and better document their economic benefits;

- Increase the diversity of our agriculture system and promote resilience in the face of environmental challenges, through public crop and livestock breeding programs and other efforts.

You and UCS: Partners for a Healthy Future

Now is the time for new policies that will level the playing field for sustainable farms and produce better, healthier food for consumers. The Union of Concerned Scientists is working to bring the best scientific and economic analysis to bear on these important policy debates, and you can help. Join our campaign and help us transform U.S. agricultural policy in ways that will ensure the growth and success of sustainable, healthy, economically robust farms.

In the Future Factory Farms Could Create Brain-Dead Chickens

Allie Compton

Allie Compton is a frontpage editor for AOL.com, an online web service. She has also written and reported for other publications.

André Ford, an architecture student from the U.K. [United Kingdom], wants to bring new meaning to the phrase "like a chicken with its head cut off."

He proposed his "Headless Chicken Solution" for a project at the Royal College of Art in which he was asked to look for sustainable solutions to the U.K.'s farming inefficiencies.

Removing Chickens' Cerebral Cortex

Currently, the U.K.'s factory farms utilize a "broiler" method to kill 800 million chickens each year for meat. The method is also popular in the U.S. where according to PETA[People for the Ethical Treatment of Animals], 7 billion chickens are raised and killed for food annually.

These chickens are typically raised in overcrowded, dark rooms. After they've grown for a few weeks, they go through a process in which an automated machines cuts their throats before dipping them in scalding water to remove feathers. But the method is imperfect, and some chickens are still conscious when dipped, while some of them miss the throat-cutter entirely.

Ford's idea is to spare chickens pain and suffering while maximizing space and production capability at the same time.

The science is simple: remove the chicken's cerebral cortex and thus remove its sense perception.

The livestock industries are responsible for 18% of all greenhouse gas emissions.

Speaking with the blog We Make Money Not Art, Ford further outlined the science behind the idea:

As long as their brain stem is intact, the homeostatic functions of the chicken will continue to operate. By removing the cerebral cortex of the chicken, its sense perceptions are removed. It can be produced in a denser condition while remaining alive, and oblivious.

Similarities to *The Matrix*

Ford told *The Huffington Post* that the inspiration for his idea came from his research, which pointed to two major issues.

"The livestock industries are responsible for 18% of all greenhouse gas emissions," Ford said in an e-mail. "This is worrying because the demand for meat is increasing worldwide and is set to double by 2050. 40% of this increase predicted to be in the poultry industry."

Architecturally, the idea would optimize space and production costs compared to current systems. He demonstrated this in his exhibition by building a honeycomb-like vertical wall of prosthetic chickens.

Ford added that he believed "the welfare provided in the existing dominant systems," including free-range farms, is "wholly inadequate."

Though the solution seeks to resolve existing poultry farming issues, it also presents a slew of new ethical dilemmas.

But, as *Wired* notes, the similarity between the idea and the horrifying dystopian future portrayed in [the movie] *The Matrix* is not lost on Ford.

"The similarities are patent, although in *The Matrix* the dominant species were kind enough to provide the subspecies with a alternate reality, which was far better than the their 'real' post-apocalyptic world," Ford told *Wired*.

But Ford insists these ethical dilemmas are inherent to the idea of raising animals for human consumption.

"Current [animal] welfare standards are a farce. 'Free range', for example, is simply a badge that alleviates the consumer from confronting the real problems inherent in eating meat," Ford told *HuffPost*. "The fact is people want to eat meat, they want to eat it as cheaply as possible, and only if they can afford it."

"Desensitization is my answer," Ford said.

His idea isn't the first attempt to find a better system than factory farming. Earlier this year *The Huffington Post*'s Cara Santa Maria reported on lab-grown "in-vitro" meat that could be available to consumers by the end of the year.

In Vitro Meat Could Soon Become a Reality

Damien Gayle

Damien Gayle is a journalist based in London, England.

Scientists have figured out the riddle of growing meat in a laboratory and are now just working out how they can make it profitable, it has been claimed.

Some 30 teams around the world are working on growing meat in petri dishes, as investment and research talent is poured into a technology that could solve world hunger.

Produced in huge vats from muscle cells, the 'meat without slaughter' would be kinder to the environment than the real thing and reduce animal suffering.

Research Efforts Underway

Animal welfare group PETA [People for the Ethical Treatment of Animals] [has] promised a $1 million reward to any scientist who can prove chicken grown in a laboratory is commercially viable by 2016.

And now a string of recent developments cited by *Food Safety News* indicate that 2012 could be the year a breakthrough is finally made in the development of in vitro meat.

Dr Mark Post, from the University of Maastricht in the Netherlands, has all but promised that meat will soon be grown in his lab.

His work is funded by the Dutch government, as well as an anonymous donation of 300,000 euros, but it is not eligible for the PETA prize as he is growing beef, not chicken.

In the U.S., meanwhile, the University of Missouri was given funding to take on Nicholas Genovese to work with R. Michael Roberts, their leading expert on stem cells and livestock.

Mr Genovese has already worked with Vladimir Mironov at the Medical University of South Carolina.

Mr Mironov has taken his research to Brazil, where the government is also pursuing in vitro meat research and development.

If an industrial process can be discovered, it is hoped that it would slash the price of test tube meat to less than that of real meat.

It remains to be seen, however, whether it will find favour with a public that likes to think of its chops, steaks and sausages as having their roots in nature, rather than in test-tubes.

And with the meaty texture of muscle being the most difficult element to recreate, it is likely that the first test-tube meat dishes would mimic processed meat products like burgers and sausages.

The In-vitro Process

To make the meat, scientists take muscle cells from an animal and incubate them in a protein 'broth'.

This makes the microscopic cells multiply many times over, creating a sticky tissue with the consistency of an undercooked egg.

This 'wasted muscle' is then bulked up through the laboratory equivalent of exercise—it is anchored to Velcro and stretched.

Some researchers say that with the right starting material and conditions, just ten pork muscle cells could produce 50,000 tons of meat in two months.

PETA has said it decided to promote lab-grown meat because a lot of people 'cannot kick their meat addictions'.

The group's $1 million prize will go to any researcher who can develop lab-grown chicken with the same taste and texture as the real thing, and sell at least 2,000 lb of the stuff in 10 American states by early 2016.

Their evaluation process deadline is in June this year [2012].

People Must Eat Less Meat

Laurie Tuffrey

Laurie Tuffrey is a journalism student at City University, London, and a frequent contributor to various websites and to The Guardian, *a British newspaper.*

A quick glance at the statistics for the environmental impact of meat production provides ample food for thought. The United Nations Food and Agriculture Organization (FAO) provides some staggering statistics. For instance, there are almost 1.4 billion cattle and 1.1 billion sheep on the planet producing 37 percent of the total methane generated by human activity, a gas that is 20 times more effective at trapping greenhouse gases than carbon dioxide. 70 per cent of all agricultural land, just under a third of the earth's entire land surface, is used for rearing farm animals. The amount of water needed to produce one kilogramme [approx. 2.2 pounds] of beef varies depending on which figures you look at, but estimates are between 13,000 litres and 100,000 litres [3,432 gallons to 26,400 gallons]. With this in mind, just how sustainable is eating meat? And if things really are as frightening as they appear, why don't more people turn to vegetarianism or even veganism?

Eating Less Meat

Animal welfare remains a primary motive for choosing a vegetarian diet and with over two million animals killed every day for food in this country, according to the Vegetarian Society, it's not hard to see why. In the UK [United Kingdom], according to a 2009 Food Standards Agency survey, around

Laurie Tuffrey, "Can Becoming a Vegetarian Help Save the Planet?" *The Ecologist*, January 4, 2012. From www.theecologist.org. This article first appeared on www.theecologist .org in January 2012.

three per cent of the population are currently vegetarian, with another five per cent regularly choosing meat-free meals. Concern for the environment, though, is also a driving factor for a number of vegetarians. "What we choose to eat," says Su Taylor, a spokesperson for the society, "is one of the biggest factors in our personal impact on the environment." The Vegetarian Society cite research by RK Pachuari, the chairman of the Intergovernmental Panel on Climate Change (IPCC), who found that one hectare [2.47 acres] of land, producing vegetables, fruit and cereals can feed up to 30 people. The same area, if used to produce meat, could feed between only five and 10.

Speaking to the *Ecologist* last year, the vegetarian American author Jonathan Safran Foer suggested a possible reason why vegetarianism isn't taken up more widely: 'People use the fear of hypocrisy to justify total inaction.' The idea that the arguments for vegetarianism lead to veganism, which can be seen as too radical a shift and stops people from making any change in their diet, is familiar to the Vegetarian Society's head of communications, Liz O'Neill. 'He puts it beautifully,' she says. 'To make a commitment to something—even if it's not the perfect answer—you are removing yourself from the damaging behaviour, from the damaging industry to whatever extent that commitment encircles. It's only by drawing a line and saying "I'm not going to be a meat-eater" that you can actually not eat any factory farmed meat.'

In the face of this, justifying eating meat from an environmental perspective can seem difficult. With factory farming the predominant means of meat production—Compassion in World Farming estimates that at least 80 per cent of the EU's farm animals are factory farmed—and a host of other issues such as overuse of antibiotics in the mix, it's becoming harder to be an ethical meat-eater. Guy Watson, the founder of Riverford Organics, an organic food box scheme delivering 40,000 boxes of vegetables, dairy and meat a week, appreciates the difficulties. "There's no doubt that in general the world would be a better place if we ate less meat and most people eat more than is good for their health and the planet's."

Problems with Animal Farming

One major problem with animal farming is the production of their feed. The crops are grown on a vast scale and combined with the space needed for cattle ranching, it accounts for the majority of the six million hectares [14,826,322 acres] of forest felled a year, according to Friends of the Earth. The inefficiency comes when crops such as soya, which could be eaten by humans, are being grown for animal feed instead. The environmental cost of this process is significant, as Watson explains: 'If you need to cultivate the grains to feed the animals, you get a massive release of carbon dioxide, whereas if you feed on permanent pasture, then it tends to accumulate and is effectively sequestering the carbon dioxide.'

Working out where the food you eat has come from is key to understanding your personal environmental impact.

Along with eating smaller portions, using more, if not all, of the animal is a far more efficient, and to some minds, respectful, way of eating meat. Having raised and killed two pigs, writer and *Ecologist* commentator Tom Hodgkinson estimates that he had over £1000 [approx. $1570] worth of meat from thoroughly butchering the animals, which were bought for £30 [approx. $48] each. For Hodgkinson, taking control of the process and reclaiming production from the large-scale producers was the far more responsible way of eating meat. 'When we had the pigs, friends would say "oh, I couldn't do it" but you can go to [the supermarket] and buy horrific Danish bacon because you've been removed from the whole process. It was quite horrible really, seeing a pig die, but we faced up to our responsibility.' . . .

So what about fish—the protein-rich fall back for many a demi-vegetarian? FAO figures show that 92 million tonnes of wild fish were landed in 2006 globally, with a further 51.6 million tonnes coming from aquaculture. According to Taylor, the latter are unsustainably inefficient. 'Fish feed is made from wild caught fish and you get just one pound of farmed fish out for every five pounds of wild caught fish you put in,' she says. While the Aquaculture Stewardship Council, the industry's monitoring body, won't be operational until later this year, the Marine Stewardship Council (MSC) currently has 134 fisheries in their programme, all of which have been certified as fishing sustainably. James Simpson, a spokesperson for the MSC, says that by carefully choosing which types we eat, sustainable fish eating is possible: 'We've just had some independent research published on the fisheries that have been certified in the MSC programme and one of the things it shows [is] an increase in stocks, so by preferencing particular sources for your fish, in this case MSC-certified, you can actually contribute to a change in the oceans, and that is an increase in the fish stocks.'

Deciding whether or not to eat meat or fish is ultimately a personal choice, although working out where the food you eat has come from is key to understanding your personal environmental impact. What remains a fact is that overconsumption of meat has significant ramifications, not only for the environment but also for our health, with a 2011 WorldWatch Institute report finding that by significantly decreasing the amount of red meat eaten, 11 percent of all deaths in men and 16 percent in women could be prevented. Eating smaller portions of ethically farmed meat is perhaps the most sustainable way of being a meat-eater, even if it means paying more. Either way, responsible meat and fish consumption is a tricky area to navigate.

Organizations to Contact

The editors have compiled the following list of organizations concerned with the issues debated in this book. The descriptions are derived from materials provided by the organizations. All have publications or information available for interested readers. The list was compiled on the date of publication of the present volume; names, addresses, phone and fax numbers, and e-mail and Internet addresses may change. Be aware that many organizations take several weeks or longer to respond to inquiries, so allow as much time as possible.

American Meat Institute (AMI)
1150 Connecticut Ave. NW, 12th Floor
Washington, DC 20036
(202) 587-4200 • fax: (202) 587-4300
website: www.meatami.com

The American Meat Institute is a national trade association that represents companies that process 95 percent of red meat and 70 percent of turkey in the United States and their suppliers throughout the United States. AMI monitors legislation, regulation, and media activity that affects the meat and poultry industry and provides rapid updates and analyses to its members. The group's website provides links, articles, testimony, and news information from an industry point of view about issues such as animal welfare, the environment, and food safety.

Animal Agriculture Alliance
2101 Wilson Blvd., Suite 916-B, Arlington, VA
(703) 562-5160
e-mail: info@animalagalliance.org
website: www.animalagalliance.org

The Animal Agriculture Alliance promotes the role of animal agriculture in providing a safe, abundant world food supply. The organization seeks to educate consumers, teachers, and the media; serves as a resource for information about animal production; monitors emerging issues; and promotes the development of animal care guidelines. The group's website includes articles and other information on issues surrounding factory farming, presented from an industry point of view. Articles that can be found there include "Animal Rights Extremists Pose an Escalating Risk to Animal Agriculture," "Antibiotics in Livestock Help Humans," and "Agriculture's Commitment to Animal Well-Being."

Center for Food Safety (CFS)
660 Pennsylvania Ave. SE, Suite 302, Washington, DC   20003
(202) 547-9359 • fax: (202) 547-9429
website: www.centerforfoodsafety.org

The Center for Food Safety is a nonprofit, public interest, and environmental advocacy membership organization established in 1997 for the purpose of challenging harmful food production technologies and promoting sustainable alternatives. CFS activities include litigation, advocacy on various sustainable agriculture and food safety issues, public education, grassroots organizing, and media outreach. The center's website contains information about food-related issues. One example is "What's Wrong with Factory Farming," a compilation of statistics about factory farming.

Center for Science in the Public Interest
1220 L St. NW, Suite 300, Washington, DC   20005
(202) 332-9110 • fax: (202) 265-4954
website: www.cspinet.org

The Center for Science in the Public Interest is an advocate for nutrition and health, food safety, alcohol policy, and sound science. The center produces the *Nutrition Action Healthletter*, and a search of its website identifies numerous articles and reports on the issue of factory farming. Examples include "Our Diet's Long Shadow," a discussion of plant versus meat foods, and "Magic Bullets Under Siege," about antibiotic resistance.

Farm Forward
PO Box 4120, Portland, OR   97208-4120
(877) 313-3276 • fax: (319) 856-1574
website: www.farmforward.com

Incorporated in 2007, Farm Forward is a nonprofit advocacy group that seeks to transform the way Americans eat and farm from the present factory farming model to humane and sustainable farming methods. The group's website offers basic information about factory farming, including sections on victories in the fight for sustainable farming and featured operations.

Farm Sanctuary
3100 Aikens Rd., Watkins Glen, NY   14891
(607) 583-2225
website: http://farmsanctuary.org

Farm Sanctuary was incorporated in 1986 as an advocacy organization for farm animals. Since then, Farm Sanctuary has conducted numerous investigations to uncover cruelty at factory farms, stockyards, and slaughterhouses; campaigned to prevent animal cruelty; and worked to encourage legal and policy reforms that promote respect and compassion for farm animals. The group also runs the largest rescue and refuge network for farm animals in North America. The Farm Sanctuary website contains a wealth of information about the negative effects of factory farming and about federal, state, and local legislative efforts to address these problems.

Humane Society of the United States (HSUS)
2100 L St. NW, Washington, DC   20037
(202) 452-1100
website: www.humanesociety.org

The Humane Society of the United States is the largest animal protection organization in the nation, and through its Farm Animal Protection campaign, it strives to take a leadership role on farm animal advocacy issues through legal means, lobbying, research, abuse investigations, and community support. The campaign's page on HSUS's website provides information about factory farming, including videos, various reports and brochures, news articles, and updates on litigation and legislation in this area. HSUS factory farming issues include "Cruel Confinement of Farm Animals," "Cruel Slaughter Practices," "Environmental Impact," "Force-Fed Animals," and "Humane Eating." The group's website provides links to news articles and other publications on these issues.

Pew Commission on Industrial Farm Animal Production (PCIFAP)
c/o Johns Hopkins Bloomberg School of Public Health, 615 N Wolfe St., Baltimore, MD 21205
website: www.ncifap.org

The independent Pew Commission on Industrial Farm Animal Production was formed to conduct a comprehensive, fact-based, and balanced examination of key aspects of the farm animal industry. On April 29, 2008, the commission issued its findings in a report, titled *Putting Meat on the Table: Industrial Farm Animal Production in America*. The report is available on the PCIFAP website, which also provides links to other reports, articles, and testimony on issues relating to factory farming.

Union of Concerned Scientists (UCS)
2 Brattle Sq., Cambridge, MA 02238-9105
(617) 547-5552 • fax: (617) 864-9405
website: www.ucsusa.org

The Union of Concerned Scientists is a science-based non-profit organization that works for a healthy environment and a safer world. UCS combines independent scientific research and citizen action to develop solutions to environmental and health problems and to secure responsible changes in government policy, corporate practices, and consumer choices. The UCS website provides information about industrial agriculture and factory farming. UCS publications include "Hidden Costs of Industrial Agriculture," "Confined Animal Feeding Operations (CAFOs) Uncovered," and "The Mounting Scientific Case Against Animal Use of Antibiotics."

World Society for the Protection of Animals (WSPA)
Nelson Tower Bldg., 450 Seventh Ave., 31st Floor
New York, NY   10123
(646) 783-2200 • fax: (212) 564-4250
e-mail: wspa@wspausa.com
website: www.wspa-usa.org

The World Society for the Protection of Animals is the world's largest alliance of animal welfare societies, with a network of more than nine hundred member organizations in over one hundred fifty countries. The group promotes animal welfare in four key areas: companion animals, farm animals, commercial exploitation of wildlife, and caring for animals affected by natural disasters. The US WSPA website contains articles about WSPA actions to protect farm animals, such as "Farm Animal Welfare Efforts Impress at Earth Summit."

Bibliography

Books

Gene Baur   *Farm Sanctuary: Changing Hearts and Minds About Animals and Food.* New York: Touchstone/Simon & Schuster, 2008.

Harvey Blatt   *America's Food: What You Don't Know About What You Eat.* Cambridge, MA: MIT Press, 2008.

Susan Bourette   *Meat: A Love Story.* New York: Penguin Group, 2009.

Jenny Brown   *The Lucky Ones: My Passionate Fight for Farm Animals.* New York: Avery/Penguin Group, 2012.

Paul K. Conkin   *A Revolution Down on the Farm: The Transformation of American Agriculture Since 1929.* Lexington, KY: University Press of Kentucky, 2008.

P. Michael Conn and James V. Parker   *The Animal Research War.* New York: Palgrave Macmillan, 2008.

Marian Stamp Dawkins and Roland Bonney, eds.   *The Future of Animal Farming: Renewing the Ancient Contract.* Malden, MA: Blackwell, 2008.

Deborah Fitzgerald   *Every Farm a Factory: The Industrial Ideal in American Agriculture.* New Haven, CT: Yale University Press, 2003.

John E. Ikerd   *Crisis and Opportunity: Sustainability in American Agriculture*. Lincoln, NE: Bison Books, 2008.

Frederick Kaufman   *Bet the Farm: How Food Stopped Being Food*. Hoboken, NJ: John Wiley & Sons, 2012.

David Kirby   *Animal Factory: The Looming Threat of Industrial Pig, Dairy, and Poultry Farms to Humans and the Environment*. New York: St. Martin's Press, 2010.

Adrian R. Morrison   *An Odyssey with Animals: A Veterinarian's Reflections on the Animal Rights & Welfare Debate*. New York: Oxford University Press, 2009.

Nicolette Hahn Niman   *Righteous Porkchop: Finding a Life and Good Food Beyond Factory Farms*. New York: HarperCollins, 2009.

Moby Park and Miyun Park, eds.   *Gristle: From Factory Farms to Food Safety*. New York: New Press, 2010.

Paul Roberts   *The End of Food*. Boston, MA: Houghton Mifflin, 2008.

Karl Weber, ed.   *Food Inc.: How Industrial Food Is Making Us Sicker, Fatter, and Poorer—And What You Can Do About It*. New York: PublicAffairs, 2009.

Periodicals and Internet Sources

American Society for the Prevention of Cruelty to Animals   "10 Ways You Can Help Fight Factory Farms," accessed February 7, 2013. www.aspca.org.

Mike Barrett   "Factory Farms Produce 100 Times More Waste than US Population," Natural Society, May 29, 2012. http://naturalsociety.com.

David Biello   "Will Organic Food Fail to Feed the World?" *Scientific American*, April 25, 2012. www.scientificamerican.com.

Mark Bittman   "The Human Cost of Animal Suffering," *New York Times*, March 13, 2012. http://opinionator.blogs.nytimes.com.

Mark Bittman   "A Chicken Without Guilt," *New York Times*, March 9, 2012. www.nytimes.com.

Cody Carlson   "The Ag Gag Laws: Hiding Factory Farm Abuses from Public Scrutiny," *The Atlantic*, March 20, 2012. www.theatlantic.com.

Megan Cross   "No Such Thing as Better Beef," Global Animal, April 17, 2012. www.globalanimal.org.

Scott Edwards   "Keeping Secrets Down on the Factory Farm," *The Huffington Post*, August 8, 2012. www.huffingtonpost.com.

Guardian   "Bigger Is Not Better in Farming,"
                      June 10, 2012. www.guardian.co.uk.

Pamela Hess   "Should We Eat Less Meat? None at
                     All?" *New York Times*, April 17, 2012.
                     www.nytimes.com.

Nicholas D.   "Where Cows Are Happy and Food
Kristof   Is Healthy," *New York Times Sunday
                     Review*, September 10, 2012.
                     www.nytimes.com.

Nicholas D.   "Is an Egg for Breakfast Worth This?"
Kristof   *New York Times*, April 11, 2012.
                     www.nytimes.com.

Maryn McKenna   "Beyond Factory Farming: Creating
                     an Appetite for Pastured Poultry,"
                     Wired, June 11, 2012.
                     www.wired.com.

James E.   "The Myth of Sustainable Meat," *New
McWilliams   York Times*, April 12, 2012.
                     www.nytimes.com.

Tom Philpott   "FDA's New Rules on Factory Farm
                     Antibiotics Are Flawed—and
                     Voluntary," *Mother Jones*, April 11,
                     2012. www.motherjones.com.

Tom Philpott   "Iowa Moves to Keep Its Factory
                     Farms Shielded from View," *Mother
                     Jones*, March 5, 2012.
                     www.motherjones.com.

Matt Ransford   "Factory Farming and Its Dire
                     Consequences," *PopSci*, March 25,
                     2008. www.popsci.com.

Andrew C. Revkin   "The Troubling Path from Pig to
                   Pork Chop," *New York Times*,
                   February 2, 2012.
                   http://dotearth.blogs.nytimes.com.

Science Daily   "Meat-Like Vegetarian Fare:
                   Replicating the Nutrition, Texture
                   and Taste of Meat and Eggs," June
                   28, 2012. www.sciencedaily.com.

Karen Steuer   "Factory Farming Series Part III:
                   Animal Waste, Waterways and
                   Drinking Water," EcoWatch, August
                   3, 2012. http://ecowatch.org.

Sabrina Tavernise "Farm Use of Antibiotics Defies
                   Scrutiny," *New York Times*, September
                   3, 2012. www.nytimes.com.

Index